The Pet Gundog Puppy

A common sense approach to puppy training

Lez Graham

Published by Trained for Life.
Copyright © Lez Graham.

First published by Trained for Life March 2013
ISBN 978-0-9570051-2-9

Photographs by Nick Ridley
Printed and bound in Great Britain

A catalogue record for this book is available from the British Library.

All rights reserved.

No part of this book may be reproduced, stored in a retrieval system, or transmitted by any means without the written permission of the author.

The information and recommendations in this book are given without any guarantees on behalf of the author who disclaims any liability with the use of this material

Contents

Foreword	ix
Acknowledgements	xi
Introduction	xiii
Please can I have a puppy..... pleeeeeze??	1
Give a dog a job	2
But it's a gundog	3
Pick a breeder, any breeder...	5
Eenie-Meenie-Minie-Mo!	7
The puppy test	8
Preparing for pup	11
Your home	11
Your garden	12
Your car	14
Your Self	14
WHAT HAVE I DONE?	15
Breathe...	17
Bringing home your puppy	17
Your puppy and other pets...	17
Hiss, Scratch, run	18
A puppy? For me? Fantastic! When is he leaving?	18
Harmony at Home	19
Not one but TWO... no!	20
Understanding your puppy	22
Way back when...	22
Thoroughly Modern Millie...	25
Birth and Beyond	28
Leaving the litter...	31
Leadership in action	32
The perfect puppy. Really? Is there such a thing?	33
The first couple of days	34
Toilet training	34
Crate training	36
Introducing a routine	38
And then some	40
Your behaviour shapes your puppy's behaviour	40
How learning takes place	41
The same but different	42
Socialisation and habituation; been there met them	42
Hey you look like me	43

Are you a dog? Really?	44
Do I know you? Are you sure?	45
Vaccinations.....	46

Training your puppy the basics: 8-12 weeks — 47
  The first week, or two — 48
    Sit — 48
    Down — 50
    Stand — 52
    The puppy recall — 53
    Walking to heel — 53
    Putting on the collar — 54
  The first month — 54
    Extending the basics — 54
    Sit — 54
    Down — 55
    Stand — 55
    Come and sit — 56
    Walking to heel — 56
    Go to heel; a.k.a. 'The Finish' — 58
    Whistle conditioning — 60
    Holding the collar and treat — 60
    Getting the lead on — 61
    Loose lead walking — 61
    Teaching your puppy to settle on his bed — 63
    Introducing the stay — 63
    Grooming — 64
    Working with a line — 65
    Playtime! — 66
  Good Manners around the home... — 67
    Feeding time — 67
    Furniture or floor? — 67
    Sit for attention — 68
    Doors and doorways — 68
    Knock, Knock — 69
    Leave it! — 71
    NO! — 73
  Safety first — 74
    Travelling by car — 74
    Stairs & steps — 75
  Help! — 75
    Jumping up — 76

Mouthing	76
Chewing things	77
The first fear period	79
And the not so basic: 12-16 weeks	80
Training exercises for your puppy	81
How to get really cool heelwork	82
Watch me!	84
Sit, down, stay or should that be wait?	85
Training the stay	86
Training the wait	88
Out and about	88
How much exercise	89
When to train... and where	89
Going for a coffee	90
Meeting a friend's dog	91
Teaching your puppy to do nothing	91
Feeding the ducks	92
Training a recall	92
Meeting strangers	94
The cone	96
Whistle sit	97
At Home	98
Not you!	98
The dreaded dishwasher	100
Just one bit of sandwich... please!	100
Sorry were you talking to me?	100
Bringing out the best in your gundog puppy: 10-16 weeks	104
Toys & balls	104
Playing fetch	104
Playing catch	106
Every retrieve is to the hand	107
The puppy retrieve	108
At home with the Adolescent: 4-6 months	110
Of being consistent, insistent and persistent	111
Taking it further...	113
Walking on a loose lead	113
Walking off lead	115
STAY!	116
There and back again	116
Halfs and quarters	117
The circle	117

Being silly 118
The feint 118
Stretching the stay 118
Recall to heel... on the move 119
Go Play 120
Long line training 122
Stop! 123
The cone 123
S-t-e-a-d-y 124
Introducing the clock 125
Two balls 126

Advancing the Adolescent Gundog: 4-6 months 127
Formalising the retrieve 127
Casting off 127
The return 129
The present 129
The finish 131
Having fun and staying safe 131
The Marked Retrieve 132
The Memory Retrieve 132
Just messing about on the river 134

Training the Teenager: 6 months plus 135
Upping the Ante 136
Introducing a thrower 136
The clock 138
The Blind Retrieve 140
Hunting in the home 141
Adding the 'get on' 142
Out and About 143
City dogs v country dogs 143

To castrate or not to castrate... that is the question 145
The Shoot and the off-shoots 146
The Shoot 146
Walked up 147
Driven 147
Beaters, Guns and Pickers-up 147
The Gamekeeper 148
Field Trials 149
Working Tests 149
Scurries 150
About the Author 151
Useful contacts 158

This book is dedicated to all of those who, like me, welcomed the glorious gundog puppy into their home.

Foreword

I have been breeding working Labradors for over 20 years and have always tried to send my puppies off to their new homes with as much information, advice and guidance as possible. Oh how I wish I had had this book to give with each and every one of them!

Whether the puppy is going to a 'working home' or as a family pet, a good grounding is so important. Nobody should think that having a puppy is a 'doddle', and at no stage does Lez shy away from how time consuming the initial training can be, however, the long term benefits are enormous.

Unlike many 'Puppy Books', Lez helps us to understand how our puppy develops from day one of its life; the transition periods before and after we acquire him, the importance of learning to communicate with your little bundle and to see life through the eyes of your puppy. The early basic training should set boundaries for years of enjoyable companionship with our dogs.

However many puppies you may have in your lifetime, each one is different and you tend to forget from puppy to puppy all the things you should, or should not, have done!!

This book sets out just about all the scenarios you may come across with your new acquisition and deals with them with a straight forward and common sense approach. Fascinating, amusing and informative, but not afraid to admit that even 'the professionals' can make mistakes; a result of which, improved timings and training methods are born.

All of which makes this book a must for both those with their first puppy and those who have been lucky enough to have had many puppies in their lifetime; we are never too old or experienced to learn!!

I have known Lez for 10 years from when she came to me for her first working Labrador – Bart, and more recently Ziggy, and have been privileged to watch her develop successful training techniques on the back of her 'behaviour' background.

I have proudly witnessed many of her 'pupils' in action both in pet homes and working environments, have participated in training sessions over the years and been grateful for her advice on numerous occasions to improve and assist with new 'members of my team'.

Her enthusiasm and good humour is infectious and this is as apparent in her writing as in real-life! How could you not want to follow all that is contained within these pages in order to have the best behaved dog in the world?

Jill Stagg
Tagtastic Labrador Retrievers

Acknowledgements

I said it when I wrote The Advanced Pet Gundog and I still feel the same; a book is written by so many more people than just the author named on the front cover.

I have had so many people who helped me with this book, not necessarily in the here and now while I've been writing it, but over the years contributing to my knowledge; the hundreds of puppy owners who have asked me to start their puppies off at home, both of the gundog variety and non-gundog; the owners of the naughty adolescent dogs that I've had the honour of putting back on the straight and narrow; and of course, all my gundoggers who train with me every week, rain or shine... and it's got to be said, we've had an awful lot of rain this year... thank you to you all.

Much appreciation has to go once more to Nick Ridley, not only for taking the most superb photos of young Ziggy but also for designing the front cover; I'm sure that my books wouldn't be anywhere near as appealing if it wasn't for his genius with the camera.

Many thanks go to Sue Jackson at Quest Gundog Training Equipment for once again supplying me with training dummies for the photo shoot and also to Ian and Jill Clinton of The Working Dog Company and Graeme Miller of Just Gundogs.

My gratitude, as always, goes to Jill Stagg for always being there to bounce ideas off and for very kindly writing the foreword to this book; I really couldn't think of anyone better or anyone I would more like to write the foreword to my puppy book... she is after all, the breeder of my Labradors and the awesome Tagtastic line.

Great thanks must be afforded to Ross McCarthy for always being there to discuss and compare training techniques; to Christine Rogers of Watamusand Golden Retrievers and Margaret Armand Smith of Oneida Cocker Spaniels, both breeders of gundogs for many years, for proof reading the section on breeding; to Mark Dawson for typesetting and artwork; to Darren Burbidge,

Jill Thorpe and Juliet Hayward for their ongoing support, as well as to David Tomlinson not only for his support for my books and methods but for the feedback that led to a more comprehensive table of contents for this book.

However, I save the greatest thanks 'til last... to my husband; for putting up with the late nights and very early mornings that my writing brings with it, for proof reading, spell checking, being honest, keeping my head out of the clouds and for making me laugh... thank you.

Introduction

Congratulations are the order of the day; either you have just got a pet gundog puppy or you're thinking of getting one... I can't think of anything nicer; a new puppy.

Well I can but there are not many things higher on the list... and very, very few, if any, once he's fully grown and trained, so congratulations on getting your puppy and congratulations for taking the first step in training him.

Most people, and I include myself with my first gundog puppy, generally don't know what they want to do with their puppy other than having 'a nice dog'. Regardless of what you want to do with your pet gundog puppy in relation to the shooting field or lying at your feet in front of the telly, the basics are the basics are the basics; whether you're looking at a Springer Spaniel, a German Short-Haired Pointer or a Labrador, especially if your gundog is indoors with you.

And what are the basics I hear you ask... oh that's easy... good manners, good obedience and a good retrieve.

And that's exactly what this book is all about; starting with "can I have a puppy?" through to the young dog being around 8 months old and about to embark on more advanced training. We'll cover everything from toilet training and crate training to stopping on the whistle and the blind retrieve.

If your puppy is well on the way to being an adolescent, and by that I mean he's four months old or older, then do yourself a favour and go for The Pet Gundog rather than this book as The Pet Gundog Puppy is, as the title says, for training the pet gundog puppy, although if you have a puppy of a different breed then this book is also for you...

Please forgive me if you have a puppy, or are planning on getting a puppy of the female persuasion, as apart from Kym, the dog that I had when I was 13, all of my dogs have been male and so I use 'him', 'he' and 'his' throughout rather than he/she, him/her and his/hers, as it would not only be incredibly tedious to write but would no doubt make for a very dull and laborious read – not exactly what I had in mind as I want to fill you full of enthusiasm to go and train your puppy, not put you to sleep.

As you read through this book please bear in mind a couple of things which will save masses of confusion later on...

I'm right handed which means my dogs walk on my left, therefore all of the exercises that I have included are for training a puppy to be on your left. If you're left handed simply swap everything over, for example when I say turn in front of your dog, I would turn left and you would turn right.

The other thing is that I tend to refer to dog treats, be they shop bought or homemade, as 'sweeties', so if you see 'give your puppy a sweetie' I don't mean a smartie I mean a dog treat. I know you're probably thinking 'you didn't need to tell me that....' all I can say is that from past experience I did.

The same also applies when I write 'Dog come' or 'Dog, blah blah blah' – in your mind, please replace 'Dog' with your dog's name.

And so, without further ado, it's time to go play with some puppies!

Please can I have a puppy..... pleeeeeze??

How many times have you heard this? Or were you the one doing the asking?

Making the decision to welcome a dog into your home is absolutely huge; the dog is a different species with different needs, and although you think you know what a responsibility it is, if it's your first dog then there's no getting away from it - it is going to be a shock to your system.

Just the amount of time involved looking after them, walking them, training them, thinking about them and generally planning your life around them - and that's before we even consider the amount of equipment we need to buy; from beds and bowls, collars and leads, toys, toys and more toys, and please, don't get me on to the amount of dog hair involved and the merits of the various hoovers on the market at the minute!

As you're reading a book titled The Pet Gundog Puppy I'm presuming it's a gundog that you either want or that you have just brought home with you.

A very wise choice in my eyes... or is it? Do you really know what you are letting yourself in for?

The gundog is an amazing companion; intelligent, biddable, trainable, powerful, good fun, good looking, has a great outlook on life and is full of savvy. Before we go any further though, please re-read the previous list... the second adjective especially; it reads 'biddable', not 'pushover'.

Many people who get a gundog as a pet (and if your dog is indoors with you, regardless of how many days shooting you have planned, he is first and foremost a pet) read pushover rather than biddable and spend the first year pulling their hair out in despair as they realise their dog is more intelligent than them, is stronger physically and mentally, and has them wrapped around his little paw; presuming they still have him that is and the dog hasn't been re-homed at 9 months after 3 gruelling 'teenage' months.

Once you've come to terms with the fact that you're going to be tripping over toys, standing in 'accidents' or 'little presents', finding chewed furniture, having soggy chewsticks stuck to the bottom of your bare feet, have dog beds in every room (downstairs), given over half of your cupboards to dog food and the other half to equipment, are going to be walking (and training) your dog every day, rain or shine, are going to be hoovering every day and picking up between two and four dog poos a day, it's time to answer the truly daunting question of 'where do I get a dog from?' A question that I must point out is getting harder and harder to answer these days.

Give a dog a job

Before we get on to that all important question, another equally important one needs to be answered first... why do you want a dog and what are you planning on doing with him? Okay, you caught me out - that was two questions rolled into one; both leading to the same thing though; breed!

Bearing in mind that the gundog group has been, over the last however many hundreds of years, bred to either find live game, to retrieve game that was shot, or both, it makes sense that you need to give them something to keep the brain, as well as the body, active – whether that is training them for what they've been bred for (which this book covers) or doing one of the other dog sports with them, agility, competition obedience and utility dog work to name just three.

If, like me with my first gundog, all you want is a really well trained companion dog at home that you can have fun with then you're in for a treat; work your way through this book and that is what you should end up with, be prepared though, once you start retrieving and training your dog in the manner he's been bred for, you'll not be able to resist training him a bit further as your bond becomes tighter and your relationship blossoms.

What about the working aspect of training a gundog? Well, the gundog group is generally split into Retrievers, Spaniels (Hunting Retrievers), Pointers and Setters and Hunt Point Retrievers (HPRs).

The Retrievers include breeds like the Labrador Retrievers, Golden Retrievers, Chesapeake Bay Retrievers, Flatcoated Retrievers, Nova Scotia Duck Tolling Retrievers... you get the idea. These are, as the name implies, the dogs that bring back the spoils, although they can be used to flush, retrieving is what's 'in their blood'.

Spaniels or Hunting Retrievers as they're referred to, include for example Springer Spaniels, Cocker Spaniels, Field Spaniels, Clumber Spaniels etc, hunt to find live game to flush, put it up to be shot and then bring it back for the table. Although the Hunting Retriever can be used to pick up, they're more often than not thought of as beaters dogs as they can get into the smaller places to put up game and retrieve game from.

The Pointers and Setters group include the English Pointer, Irish Setters, Gordon Setters and so on. The Pointers and Setters have their origins very much in England, Scotland and Ireland. Their job is to find game, freeze or point at it until instructed to either flush or allow their handler to deal with it.

The Hunt Point Retrievers (HPRs) are generally European dogs that became more popular after the second world war and include German Short-haired Pointers, Italian Spinones, Large Munsterlanders, Vizlas, Weimaraners and so on.

The Pointers and Setters and the HPR group, although having different origins have similar roles on the shooting field, and really come into their own working on the expansive grouse moors.

Please don't think for a minute that if you want to go picking up you have to have a Labrador as you don't, likewise with beating; it's not restricted to breed, rather to ability and level of training. I know many spaniels that are excellent picking up and peg dogs and labradors that go beating.

The shoot and its various components, as well as Working Tests, Certificates and Field Trials will be covered later as I don't want to bog down this very important part of the book with shooting terminology; however, now that you know what the different groups have a penchant for you can look at the breeds within them.

But it's a gundog

It's really important that you know what the breed that you've chosen for your family has been bred to do as it will give you a good idea, hopefully, of what you can expect; while the breed standards that the Kennel Club produce are very good and cover some of the temperament of the breed, the best thing that you can do before choosing the breed that will lie at your feet for the next ten years or so, is to talk to people.

The breed standard for example, makes very little differentiation between the Cocker Spaniel and the Working Cocker Spaniel as they are classed as one breed, however, they really are worlds apart. The description of 'a busy little dog' is so understated, especially of the working 'type' and if you get one with Field Trial Champions (FTCh) in their immediate lineage, then you're in for an explosion of energy and I really wouldn't recommend them for the first time dog owner.

It's not just the working cocker, which I use as an example, but any breed that has lots of FTCh in their lineage; please, please think twice about investing in one of these for your first dog, especially if both of its parents are, save it until you understand the psyche of the gundog and until you're ready for a full on dog otherwise you might find yourself 'over dogged' and looking for suitable homes when he hits the teenage months, if not earlier.

It's not all doom and gloom with the gundog breeds, honest. For me, you can't beat a gundog; show type or working type, they were all bred to work at some point. Even my flouncy blonde 'show type' golden retriever can do a good days work on the field; it's down to training and ability rather than 'type', however, the working 'type' have been bred for speed and stamina which is why they don't always make the best first time gundog.

Although some breeds are classed as being more intelligent than others, just like with humans, individuals learn at their own pace. Generally speaking, the larger the breed the slower they are to mature which does have an impact on their learning ability; the 'working types' do tend to be quicker on the uptake which isn't always a good thing as they need more mental simulation, and so the tendency is to over exercise when young, meaning the levels of exercise they need as an adult is phenomenal.

Which breed to bring home is a major decision and one that needs to be taken by the adults in the family, not the children; I once recommended the rehoming of a 12 week old Bernese Mountain Dog, not only was it very inbred with 'issues' but it was totally unsuitable for the family. Why did they choose this breed? Because their four year old daughter wanted one to go with the fluffy toy one that she took everywhere with her! Need I say any more?

When choosing your breed, look for health, temperament, care and maintenance and looks, preferably in that order, however, be honest with yourself and, if like for me, looks are important, start there. There's absolutely no point what so ever looking at the retrievers or the pointing breeds if long, soft, fluffy 'spaniel' ears do it for you.

Once you've decided on the breed or type of dog that you want, and that fits in with your lifestyle, then the mammoth task of finding one that fits you and your family is underway.

Pick a breeder, any breeder...

Acquiring a puppy way back when was much easier than it is now; you knew someone who had a litter or you knew someone whose mate had had a litter. My first dog came from my sister, my second I rescued as a puppy from a home who couldn't toilet train him and so he was going to get put to sleep; next it was my first pedigree - Bart a black Labrador.

I fell in love with his half brother and went on a quest (once hubby agreed to a dog that is) to get the same or similar breeding, then whilst living in New Zealand a litter of Golden Retrievers was recommended to me and lastly I returned to Bart's breeder to get his nephew.

All very straight forward but what if I hadn't fallen in love with the little black Labrador puppy? How would I have found a dog once we'd decided that we were going to have one?

The best place to start is always word of mouth recommendation, either by seeing a friend's dog and liking the temperament or seeing a dog working on a shoot or at a gamefair; a quick warning about gamefair demonstration dogs, they are generally kennelled dogs, trained by extremely experienced trainers and have had two to three years training; they did not arrive trained, a lot of hard work has gone into them – a silly warning perhaps but I've seen many dogs rehomed after owners expected them to be at the same level as the gamefair dogs after six months!

The Kennel Club website (see useful contacts) provides vast amounts of information for people looking to buy pedigree puppies. By typing in the breed that you're interested in you are able to choose from breeders in your area by clicking on regions of a map; you can then read about litters that have been registered with the Kennel Club and when they'll be available.

The Kennel Club also operate The Assured Breeder Scheme which is about promoting good breeding practices; remember though that just because a breeder isn't part of this scheme doesn't mean they're not good and responsible breeders, it just means that they're not a member of the scheme.

Another great source of information for pedigree puppies are the breed clubs. I always recommend that you contact at least three breeders, and as well as asking them about their breeding lines, ask them about the other breeders that you may be interested in; you may just get a fuller picture.

Although I know lots of very good pedigree dogs that aren't registered with the Kennel Club, personally I would be wary of getting a pedigree that isn't KC registered. Why go to the expense of purchasing a pedigree dog without that final piece of paper; it may come back and haunt you later depending on what activities you want to do with your dog, activities that at the time of picking up your little bundle of fluff you didn't even know existed.

Puppy farming is rife, dealing with pedigrees and the new designer cross-breeds, the cockapoo, springador, sprocker and so on. Unfortunately they're very canny and come up with all sorts of tricks to lead the trusting public astray... and the excuses are plenty – "oh my wife has just taken the mum out for a walk"; "oh she gets a little bit nervous around strangers"; "I can't find the photo of the sire – must have mislaid it"; "take two puppies as one on its own will be lonely"; "I only have two puppies left and it's not fair to only take one".

Absolutely insist on seeing the dam, with her puppies and stroke them around her. Ask to see a copy of the sire's pedigree and at the very least a photograph of him, preferably with the owner and preferably with the dam so at least you know they got together at some point.

Dogs do get sick in their lifetime and many factors contribute to the wellness of a dog – it's not always down to breeding, just like with us it can be down to lifestyle and diet. However, it is imperative that the dam and sire (mam and dad) have been health screened according to what is prevalent in that breed, for example with Spaniels it's hips and eyes; Labradors it's hips, elbows and eyes (see The Kennel Club website's health information for each breed to see which tests are mandatory and which are recommended).

Although running the tests on the parents is no guarantee that your new puppy won't have any problems, you at least know he's got the best chance of having a clean bill of health.

You're now at the stage where you have a list of breeders to phone, which will be quickly reduced down to a list of breeders to go visit alongside a list of questions ranging from 'has she had a litter before? Did you keep any of the puppies? Can I see them?', 'will the puppies be Kennel Club registered?', 'will their tails be docked (if working spaniels)?' all the way through to 'can I give one a cuddle?', some you will want to ask over the phone, others you'll want to ask before you see the puppies, while you're with the puppies and when you get home.

Easy to say, but don't be pressured to making a decision there and then, especially in the times of the mobile phone; have a think and then give them a ring – even if it's just five minutes down the road!

Please take a deep breath and walk away from the following; dirty kennels, unkempt dirty looking bitch, growly bitch, bitch not in attendance with puppies, breeder arranging to meet up at services and having puppies in the back (with or without bitch this will be a puppy farmer), 2-3 other unrelated breeders advising against the line, hereditary diseases, aggression within the line, lack of health checks; it may save you years of heart ache.

Bear in mind though, that the bitch will be feeding the puppies solely until the breeder helps by supplementing food at three to four weeks so if you visit around this time the bitch may look a bit on the slim side, especially if it's a large litter; visit again a couple of weeks later and her condition should have seriously improved, if not, walk away.

Eenie-Meenie-Minie-Mo!

So, you've found your breeder, they tick all of the boxes for you and you tick all of the boxes for them, you love the mum and the pups are adorable; you now have the unenviable task of choosing your puppy!

Where to start? Well if you have your heart set on a certain sex that rules out the some of the litter straight away. What about colour? Is colour important? If you want a black boy and there's only one then that's it, job done, but what if there's seven black boys to choose from?

Although there are ways of testing puppies, my advice is, and always will be, give the breeder a list of what you're looking for in your dog and let the breeder choose for you. Why?

Well what you see on your visits, and you should visit more than once, are snapshots into your puppy's life. You might be looking for a quiet little chap and think that the docile puppy, snoozing over there with his mates is perfect for you, much more suitable than the one that is trying to pull your laces to bits; however, that docile puppy might, five minutes earlier, have been terrorising all the other puppies and has fallen asleep out of exhaustion whereas the one chewing your laces has just woken up, is feeling good and is up for a little adventure before he has another wee snooze.

Your breeder however, will be spending any spare time they have looking after the puppies, fussing over them and generally hanging out with them and the dam and will know all their personalities, and, by the time they are four or five weeks old, what kind of dog they'll be likely to turn into.

Remember though that you want your breeder to chose the potential dog for you and your family not for themselves; if the breeder trials their dogs and says "if it was me I would have that one", then unless you're going to do some serious work with your dog, it would probably be best for the breeder to keep him and you take his 'number two' on the list.

The puppy test

Some people say testing puppies is an art, others that it's a waste of time. For the tests to have any kind of meaning you would need to do them the first time you meet the puppies and at around 6 to 8 weeks old. This, for me, is another reason why I don't put much store in them and always go on breeder recommendation; ideally you would want to see the puppies before they were around four weeks old and revisit them a couple of times if at all possible; also, if the breeder has been doing their job right, all of the puppies by this age will be so used to being handled, played with and following people around that the tests are pretty much irrelevant.

Whenever possible an expert in the breed would be used as the full testing process includes squeezing toes and putting pressure on the puppy; if you want your puppy tested then ask an expert who is experienced in puppy testing to go with you when the puppies are about 7 weeks old, this means that you will be able to have been visiting with the puppies a couple of times and won't be a stranger to them, although your tester will be.

Bear in mind though, that by the time you've seen the litter a few times, your heart will belong to a particular puppy, and, if the litter is sought after, they will all have been chosen. There's no reason why, with your breeders permission, you can't incorporate a 'gentler' version of the tests whilst you're cooing over the puppies. Although the main thing is to make it as stress free as possible for the puppy, you will need to remove him from the litter for the test, as to not do so is putting too much pressure on the puppy to 'perform' when the lure of his siblings is close to hand.

It's important to remember that all you're looking for with these gentle tests are levels of annoyance, the more easy going the puppy the less they will display it, whereas a naturally high ranking puppy may display annoyance the longer the test goes on for; is it a reason not to get the puppy? Possibly, it depends on the level of annoyance displayed; if in doubt repeat the tests on a different day and at a different time of day.

Use these as a way of raising your awareness of the puppy you're going to take home rather than basing your decision on them, to do that you really need to get an expert involved and, as well as doing the full testing procedure, draw on his years of experience handling and training the breed.

Up and over
Lift your puppy up by interlinking your hands underneath and suspending him a couple of inches off the ground; the puppy should stay reasonably relaxed.

Readjust your hold, so the puppy is comfy, and gently lift him up and turn him over. You don't have to hold him at arm's length, you can do this whilst cuddling him and giving him a tummy rub; the puppy should relax or stay relaxed.

Being turned over shouldn't be an issue; mum will have been flipping her puppies over with her nose from the minute they were born, however, as they get a bit older, start asserting themselves and finding their position in the litters pecking order, they may object.

You guessed it; the softer more malleable pup will be the one that relaxes against you.

The toe rub
Take your puppy's front paws gently in your hands, lift them an inch, so the puppies weight is on his hind end, and give them a wee rub for a couple of seconds; most puppies will struggle to some degree, some may try to mouth to try and get you to let go, all perfectly natural and acceptable; what isn't acceptable though is throwing a tantrum, growling, glaring at you and really biting at your hands.

If they do, there's a very good chance that this puppy is going to have some temperament problems or the breeder hasn't done their job right in relation to handling the puppies sufficiently; either way, if you're new to dogs I would get a second opinion before you take this puppy home with you.

Chase and Fetch
This is just that; chase and fetch. Take a little toy with you, a bit of sheepskin works a treat or a little ball on a rope, wriggle it around to get the puppy interested and throw it a couple of feet away from you; hopefully the puppy will chase it and pick it up, with encouragement, silliness and a bit of luck, the puppy should come bounding back for you to throw it again.

The noise
As the puppy runs past you make a funny noise, reasonably loudly; funny not scary. The puppy should turn to look at you; look with interest that is, not glare at you or run away from the noise. The more confident puppy will come over to investigate, the more dominantly natured will turn and glare.

The puppy testing is an interesting process to try, it may raise foibles about the puppy that you're planning on taking home, however, what mainly happens, is we fall in love with a pair of brown eyes, blue if we see the puppies early enough, and no amount of testing is going to change that.

Preparing for pup

Once you've chosen your little bundle of fluff and fun, it's time to book a couple of weeks off work and blank out a couple of pages in your diary; you really are going to have to put your life on hold for the next two to three weeks.

Before your puppy arrives though, there are a few things that you need to get organised first, sorry did I say a few? I meant a hundred and one...

Your home

One of the most effective ways to puppy-proof your home is to invest in a crate: and I said 'crate', not 'cage'. Many people are put off getting crates for their puppy as in their mind they read 'cage', but trust me, it is the easiest way not only to puppy-proof your home but to toilet train – and to keep your sanity. Look on the crate as a den, a refuge and a place of safety for your puppy; before you know it they'll be putting themselves to bed, but I get ahead of myself.

Try to get a smaller crate to start off with as if it's too large your puppy may want to use one end as a toilet, so either get a smaller cheap crate to start off with or invest in one that comes with a divider that you can move as the puppy grows.

Place your crate in the room that you're likely to be in most once the puppy arrives and try to place it fairly close to the 'toileting' door. If your kitchen is big enough this tends to be the best place, or the utility room if you have one, or the dining room, or, if you work from home, your office providing it's near an outside door, otherwise consider temporarily moving your office... it really does depend on your lifestyle as to where you place your crate.

Drape a single bed sheet over the crate so that it can cover the top and three sides down to the ground; if you can match it with the colour of the room it will blend in, look more like it belongs rather than a 'cage', you'll feel comfortable putting your puppy in it, and most importantly, it will feel like a den to the puppy, which, if left to their own devices, is where the mum would have wanted to have given birth.

Walk around the rooms and check that there are no trailing cables or anything sticking up that the puppy may find super interesting; if your carpet has started to come up from the skirting or the runner, now is the time to fix it as I guarantee that if you don't your puppy 'will'.

Now, get down on your hands and knees and look at the rooms from your puppy's perspective; it looks very different doesn't it?

You may wish to invest in a stair gate for the room, or you may not; if you're crate training then it's highly unlikely you'll need one, especially if you heed the advice that follows.

As well as your crate you'll need some vet bed, which is hopefully what your breeder has used, it's the white fluffy stuff with a green back; perfect for drawing those little accidents away from your precious little bundle and it washes up fantastically. Three is the ideal, one in the crate, one spare and one in the wash; no doubt this sounds familiar if you're a parent.

I would also recommend that you get a bowl that attaches to the inside of the crate, sometimes known as a coup cup; that way the bowl is secure and is lifted ever so slightly off the ground so if the puppy gets a bit boisterous with his toys the bowl isn't going to be toppled.

You may also want to invest in a 'snugglesafe' which is a hard plastic disc that can be heated up in the microwave and put under the vet bed so your puppy has something to snuggle down against. You can also get wonderful covers for them which are big floppy puppies that you put the snugglesafe inside of – the chunky legs are perfect for your puppy to lie up against and may help him feel less homesick when he first comes home.

Your garden

There are many hazards in the garden that you need to check for, however, I'm not going to give you a list of plants to avoid planting or that need taken out.

Google 'poisonous plants for dogs' and you'll get a comprehensive list, not only that, it means your list is always up to date, unlike a book which is out of date the second it is sent to the printers; if you don't have a computer at home then pop down to the local library and ask the librarian to help you do this - if my memory serves right it will only cost the price of a standard photocopy or it may even be a donation for the printing cost.

Check your fences; do they go all the way to the ground? If not invest in some wire to take them down to the ground and consider placing a little on the ground as well before securing, that way puppy won't be able to wriggle under when you're not looking. Are there any gaps? You'll be amazed at what a puppy, especially the smaller breeds, can get through. If in doubt put wire over it until the puppy has grown up.

Check your hedges; any gaps at all and your puppy will be through. As with the fences, if you find any gaps then put chicken wire there to prevent puppy wriggling though when you're not looking... and I say not looking, as you'll read later, a puppy should never be unattended and left to his own devices, so while puppy proofing your garden is really important, it's more about escape routes as the rest of the time your puppy will be supervised.

Do you have steps and walls? I remember when Angus was a puppy, we had a drop down into the garden of about 12 inches and he would want to leap off there like a polar bear launching itself off an ice floe; he thought it was great fun, and it was, but it didn't stop my heart leaping when he did it. Try as I might, the second he got the chance he was going for it, in the end I stopped trying to stop him and just monitored the amount of time he was in the back garden until he was 4 months old.

A single step isn't so bad providing that, unlike Angus, they don't launch themselves off it, and that they are landing on a soft surface, however, multiple steps are dangerous; not only will they be hard landing but the repeated bounce, bounce, bounce down them will jar your puppy's little elbow joints which is something to be avoided at all costs. Also a young puppy hasn't got the greatest co-ordination and sense of balance, so may end up putting too much weight over their front end and topple tail over head down them.

If you have steps in your garden cordon them off until your puppy is older and more in control; in terms of co-ordination, basic obedience and good manners.

Do you have a pond? If so cover it up and fence around it; try to treat the arrival of your puppy as you would the arrival of a toddler or a baby that is crawling – into everything and everything into their mouth, so as you're inspecting your garden (and your home) try to think toddler-proof as well as puppy-proof.

Your car

Safety in the car is so important, not only for your puppy but for us also, and, apart from the journey home which I always recommend is on a passenger's lap, the best way for a puppy to travel is in a crate.

Not only will the crate keep your puppy safe in the event of an accident, but it will stop him from being thrown around the car at speed when you go around bends; it will also keep your car intact when you leave your puppy in it. As your puppy gets older you may want to invest in a dog guard/tail gate but initially you just cannot beat a crate.

Your Self

Probably the most important thing of all is preparing yourself for the arrival of your puppy. If you've had puppies before then you kind of know what you're letting yourself in for, although no two puppies are the same and we humans are great at looking at the past through rose tinted glasses… every single person I know who gets a puppy always say that they forget how much hard work and time consuming it is in the early days.

You literally won't have time to turn around let alone socialise – be prepared to put your life on hold for 2-3 weeks after the puppy comes home as you'll be shattered. Honestly, I'm not exaggerating – think of it as bringing home a new baby; just a new baby of a different species who hasn't got a clue as to what's going on, is in an alien world, is very, very dependent on you and whom you cannot take your eyes off for a minute.

Mentally you need to prepare for the responsibility that dog ownership entails. Remember that when you take on a dog it really is for life, or at least that's how it should be approached.

You will need to make all of the decisions for your puppy and, as he matures, for your dog. One of the biggest responsibilities for a dog owner is sticking to the unspoken bond between you and the puppy that you bring home that you will always do your best by them, that you will not let them suffer unnecessarily, and that you will be brave enough to do 'the deed' in a timely manner when it arrives… timely, that is, for your dog, not for you.

WHAT HAVE I DONE?

At some point, more than likely in the next couple of weeks, if not in the next couple of days, you're going to be thinking to yourself "what have I done?"

I know I did within weeks of bringing home Bart, my first gundog, and within a week of bringing home Angus, my Goldie.

Why? Well things are so different when you're a 'grown up' and you have to do it all. I got my first dog Kym when I was 13 and she was my mate... I did all of the training and hanging out together, she used to walk me half way to school and was there to meet me on the way home to carry my school bag. I taught her tricks galore including how to shake hands, play dead, commando crawl and jump with a raw egg in her mouth without cracking it.

My mam dealt with the unpleasantries of house training, good manners around the home, clearing up sick and poo when Kym was poorly and organised the buying of food, feeding and so on.

My second dog, Sabre, was a puppy that I rescued from being put to sleep. I was 18, lived in a flat and had absolutely no responsibilities. I retrained him so that he could join a young family and always had that in mind when I took him on so had a different mindset with him.

With Bart however, and then with Angus, I had a young family to look after, was self employed and looked after my household. Bart was a great puppy, surprisingly easy, although bearing in mind he had a great breeder who worked at socialising him and habituating him to things around the house and general manners, it's not surprising. However, I didn't use a crate and didn't even restrict him to one room – as for a stair gate, well that didn't enter my head. Imagine my horror on my first morning after bringing him home to find he'd wee'd and poo'd all over the sitting room, kitchen and hall.

That was when I discovered crate training and things got an awful lot easier even as I became sleep deprived with the routine of it and looking after a family. After only ever seeing the nice side of young puppy ownership however, Bart was a shock to the system.

Angus, I thought I was prepared for but I was wrong. It was at this point that I realised the true value of Bart's breeder – Angus was raised on a 15 acre vineyard in New Zealand and from the age of five to six weeks was given free rein to do as he pleased along with his siblings. He was also kept in a large carpeted room that had newspaper placed down, unfortunately the breeder wasn't quick at replacing the paper which meant the puppies were toileting onto carpet.

You've guessed it haven't you? Yup, Angus thought that the 'done thing', in fact the 'only thing', was to toilet on carpet; it didn't matter how long I kept him outside for he would toilet the second his paw touched carpet.

And that wasn't the worst part. Because he'd been given free rein he couldn't settle and would howl constantly if he was away from us; even if I left him with Bart he would howl. He would howl for three hours, sleep for twenty minutes and then howl again... all night long. It went on for almost four weeks and I still get that sinking feeling when I think back to those days – you may not be surprised to know that Angus was known as the puppy from hell.

Breathe...

Before we go any further take a deep breath; I included my experiences above with my dogs, and will do so throughout about mine and various client's dogs, both good and bad, so you don't feel alone in what you're going through.

Sometimes it's easier to learn by reading about other people's experiences rather than being told to do this and do that, especially as every situation is as different as every puppy; that's not to say some things aren't universal, like training the sit etc., but for others they're very personal and individual.

Getting a puppy is a massive commitment and incredibly scary, your life is never going to be the same again, in a good way I hasten to add, although in the early days you may well yearn back for the puppy free days.

Hopefully it won't be this way for you and, to instil some hope, Ziggy, the two year old black Labrador at my feet has been excellent; his only thing is that he's incredibly intelligent and has at times been hard to keep up with.

Bringing home your puppy

Organise to bring your puppy home as early as possible in the day and midweek when the children are at school, that way you'll more or less have the puppy settled before they come home; by arranging the homecoming mid-week you won't have the trauma of the first weekend with the children before you establish a puppy routine.

Wherever possible organise the person, and by that I mean the adult, who the puppy is for, to be a passenger so that they can cuddle the puppy all the way home. Why? Well your puppy has just left the only security he knows and by cuddling into you in the car by the time you get home your puppy will be saturated with your smell (and please don't wear strong smelling perfume/deodorant/aftershave, we want the puppy to know you, the 'real you') and your scent will be all over the puppy. Your puppy will associate you as their refuge when entering the scary world of the unknown and your bond will more or less be sealed.

Take a large towel, a lot of kitchen roll and some poo bags for the journey home and have your puppy snuggle into the towel; if he's poorly just fold it into the towel, or if you can do it without causing too much fuss a bit of kitchen roll.

Make your journey last at least twenty minutes, so if you're just around the corner go for a couple of laps around the block so that you can really bond with your puppy on the way home.

Once you're home, carry your puppy into the garden, place him gently on the ground and settle down with him while he stretches his legs and hopefully goes to the toilet. Then it's into the kitchen (or wherever you have the crate set up) to sit on the floor and just 'be' with your puppy making sure that access to the rest of the house is closed off. Don't try to feed him straight away as he'll be a little disorientated from his journey, just 'hang out' with him and be prepared to feed him at his usual time.

Your puppy and other pets...

Introducing your puppy to other pets in the house should be relatively straight forward, although you can never tell, especially with cats.

If you have a dog at home already, please don't present the puppy to him as soon as you get home. Instead keep them separate for 24 hours; that means separate rooms and dividing your time and energies; either the puppy is with you or your established dog is with you, but not both.

The reason why this is recommended is so that the puppy has the first 24, or 48 hours, just with the humans in the house and will look to you first; dogs will always bond first with other dogs given half a chance, and from experience, if you keep the puppy separate for 24 hours the puppy will be yours, not your dogs.

Hiss, Scratch, run

The best way to introduce your new puppy to your resident cat is to not; just allow the cat to do its usual thing and encourage him into the room whilst the puppy is in the crate so that the cat feels safe around the puppy. Any kind of bounding after or chasing of the cat is to be strictly forbidden; more on that later when we cover good manners.

I can remember quite clearly, and very naively, introducing Bart to my resident cat, a huge Maine Coon called Charley. My husband was holding Charley and I was holding Bart; I held Bart towards Charley to meet him, which was the same way as I'd introduced Kym my first dog to my horse with great success. Well, Charley threw a fit, he sank his claws straight into my hubby, ran up his chest and bounced of his shoulder, all the while hissing with his tail fluffed up like a big bottle brush... "Hmm, that went well then!"

We then allowed Charley to do his own thing and monitored Bart, within a week they good friends; not always the case but patience and a bit of common sense is generally all that is called for, certainly more common sense than I displayed introducing Bart.

A puppy? For me? Fantastic! When is he leaving?

I brought Angus home after a ten minute car journey, walked into the living room where Bart was and popped him down; from that moment, until Angus was about 8 months old, Angus was Bart's dog.

The first couple of days after Angus arrived Bart was in doggy heaven; he had a playmate and another dog to hang out with. Within a week however he had had enough of having a blonde shadow and was desperate for some time with me; after being an only dog for nearly three years he was really feeling it, all bad management on my part I hasten add. The fact that Angus really was the puppy from hell didn't help matters at all.

It's another reason why I recommend you divide your time between your puppy and your resident dog. Even after the first twenty four hours you'll need time when your puppy is in his crate and your resident dog is 'hanging out' with you, going on walks, training or just relaxing at your feet.

Harmony at Home

By the time I introduced Ziggy into the family I'd had many years experience 'starting off' puppies, that is going into client's homes and giving advice on all things puppy related, and so, as you would expect, bringing in another puppy was relatively straight forward.

We collected Ziggy early in the morning, had a two hour drive home then all sat in the garden for half an hour or so to give Ziggy a chance to toilet. Angus in the meantime was in the living room where he could neither see nor be seen (we didn't have Bart, Ziggy's uncle, by this time; he died a week to the day after Ziggy was born).

I then took Ziggy through the patio doors into my office which is where his crate lives and we sat on the big dog bed and bonded. It was almost 48 hours before I introduced him to Angus by quite simply allowing Angus into the office one day when Ziggy was in his crate. I let Ziggy out of his crate after Angus had 'inspected' him through the bars and that was that.

Although Angus and Ziggy have a much closer and 'touchier' relationship than Bart and Angus had, that is they sleep cuddled up together, quite often choosing to lie in the same crate, Ziggy is very much my dog and is totally focused on me which is down to, I believe, the first 48 hours of him leaving his litter.

Not one but TWO... no!

Don't do it, don't get two get one!

Please, please, please don't be tempted to get two puppies at the same time. You might think that's no big deal, just a bit more work; but it isn't. It is much, much more; more than double the amount of work; double the amount of equipment; double the amount of storage and unfortunately double the amount of heartache.

No self respecting breeder would sell two litter mates to the same person, or even two puppies of the same age from different litters to the same person as they know what's involved once you get them home; the unscrupulous breeder however, will and you'll receive comments like "oh there's only one puppy left and they'll be lonely on their own", "these two were inseparable, it would be awful if you left one behind", "they'll settle much quicker if you take more than one" and so on… anything to get rid of the puppies so they're not left with them.

As a behaviourist I see many people who are at their absolute wits end as they got two puppies at the same time; the fortunate ones call me early on and are happy to either rehome one or send them both back to the breeder, the unfortunate ones have bonded with both puppies and refuse to give one up.

Why such a big deal? Well, as well as having time individually with each puppy you'll want time with them together, only about 10-15 minutes at a time a few times a day though as they'll end up squabbling and bonding with each other and disregard you. Oh yes, and then you'll need puppy free time as well.

You'll have to juggle toilet training; on an individual basis as you can't take your eyes off your puppy for an instant; likewise with juggling basic training, which you should be doing, ideally, at least three or four times a day; then you have your good manners around the home whilst 'hanging out' with you, again individually so that you teach them how to behave in the human world… and this doesn't stop when they're toilet trained.

You can't train two dogs to walk nicely on a loose lead at the same time so, until the puppies are approximately eight months old you'll be walking them separately, and at eight months that's about half an hour, twice a day – each!

Have I put you off yet? No? okay, here's two stories based on past experiences.

I received a phone call about five years ago from a lady who had bought two beagles from the same litter; why beagles? No idea... anyway, after the first day she thought they were going to kill each other as all they did was fight. My first question to her was "how attached are you to the puppies"; well she'd got one for each of her children and she didn't want to disappoint them. After talking her through the above, in depth and in very plain language, she realised she'd made a mistake and very, very wisely, took them back to the breeder.

Six months later she phoned and asked for advice in relation to which breed for her family and which breeders I could recommend. She now has a wonderful Springer Spaniel which is an absolute delight for her and her family.

I received another phone call probably about six months after the 'beagle' lady and a couple of months after Christmas. A man had presented his wife, on boxing day would you believe, with not one, but two boxer puppies; and then promptly started working abroad mid-week only coming home on weekends, leaving his wife, quite literally 'holding the puppies'.

Do yourself, your puppy and your stress levels a favour, and only get one puppy at a time.

Understanding your puppy

Before we get into the how to do this and how to do that, it's really important that you understand a bit about the bundle of fluff that's on your lap or curled up in his crate. As the more intelligent of the two in the relationship, the being that is a master of learning languages and most importantly the being that is in charge, it's up to us to learn what it means to be a dog, or a *Canis lupus familiaris*, to give it its proper name.

Why? well not only will it make it easier for you to train your puppy but it will make it easier for your puppy to understand what it is you want; your puppy will never understand the spoken or the written word, the format of the brain doesn't allow it – all of the words your puppy will ever learn will be through consistent conditioning.

They also have to learn how to read our body language and facial expressions, in the same way they learned how to speak 'dog' with their mum and litter siblings, so too they have to learn 'human' and in order to help them to do so we need to be expansive in our facial expression and consistent in our body language and spoken word.

Just imagine that you were put into a non-removable burka and dropped into rural China, where funnily enough, everyone else was wearing non-removable burkas and not one of them spoke English, not only that but all of the signs were in Chinese; that is kind of what you've done to your puppy by taking him out of his world and placing him in yours.

Now don't go feeling sorry for him, rather step up to the mark and be the leader your puppy not only needs, but thoroughly deserves.

Way back when...

In the days when the *Canis lupus familiaris* was still a *Canis lupus*, a wolf, the two most senior ranks would get together to breed. The offspring from the current and previous litters (that hadn't moved on to join other packs) are what would have made up the wolf pack.

The structure of the wolf pack isn't that dissimilar from a human family with Alpha Male and Alpha Female running the show, followed by the Beta animal, the second in command who at times will take the lead (on the behest of the pack leader) and may also be the disciplinarian... think of this role as the eldest child in the human family helping out the folks, looking after the younger brothers and sisters and laying the table etc.,

There's then the middle and senior ranks, which is where a lot of the fluidity in the wolf pack lives as the tussling for the better positions and bits of food takes place. And finally there is the lowly omega rank, the lowest position of all, the position that takes the flak when the pack is having a bad day and the one that will put itself forward to take the flak should emotions run high between two senior/middle ranking animals.

There may be an occasional interloper that has been allowed to join the pack, however, for the most part, the pack is made up of siblings.

As well as the 'top down' hierarchy, there's also a ranking structure for the males and a ranking structure for the females, just as there is in human families. What's interesting (and hopefully you'll be nodding your head in agreement) is that the male hierarchy is pretty much stable, once you have your position in life you're kind of happy with it, whereas with the females it's a different picture entirely and the ranking structure can be quite fluid depending upon the individuals hormone levels at any particular time... it's not unusual for a senior ranking male to defer to a 'hormonal' lower ranking female – and who can blame him, eh?

Hunting and mealtimes is a very ordered affair with the pack leaders organising the troops with regard to strategy, positioning and which animal to bring down; all done silently and stealthily with communication primarily being through the gaze and body language – not unlike the silent communication that human soldiers use.

Once the animal (or animals) is killed, the leaders will either eat their fill at the carcass or tear a piece off and slope off to eat in peace; the Beta will be in charge of calming the ranks as the bloodlust will be upon the pack and this is when scuffles are likely to break out... if you have experience of having more than one dog you'll see a watered down version of this as the dogs play fight and bound around whilst waiting to be fed. When the leaders (including the Beta rank) have walked away from the kill the rest of pack tuck in, eating their piece of meat according to rank; the higher the rank the better the meat, the lower the rank the less desirable piece, maybe a tail or a hoof.

Once the pack is finished eating then a general cleaning up takes place of themselves and each other, with a higher rank quite often cleaning up a lower rank although sometimes the leader will indulge a lower rank cleaning them... then its playtime! The pack know that it's survived another day, that the pressure of finding dinner is over and so the animals can relax and have a good old frolic, chasing each other around and mock fighting.

Playtime is really important for the wolf pack as not only is it a way of letting off steam and bonding with other pack members, but it is when the hierarchy of the pack is often decided... the wolves know that there's absolutely no point whatsoever of making a challenge against a higher ranking wolf that cannot be brought down in play. To make a claim for a rank against a wolf that is unbeatable in play when the bloodlust is high from a kill is tantamount to suicide and no wolf, other than the Omega, will deliberately put itself or the pack in danger (which is why there's generally no aggression 'issues' in the natural kingdom).

Sleeping, like everything else in the life of the pack, is an ordered affair, with the senior ranks close to the leaders and the lowest ranks on the outside; this tends to change to the Beta animal on the outside if the pack is migrating across unfamiliar territory then, rather than having the least important on the outside, the leader's bodyguard is there keeping sentry watch to ensure that the pack survives another day.

Breeding is the privilege of the Alpha Male and Alpha Female only; also termed as the breeding pair. Only the fittest can pass on their genes and as Alpha Male and Alpha Female that is exactly what they are. The only exception to this is if the pack is very small and the area is abundant in which case the Alpha Male may mate with another senior ranking female to boost the pack's numbers, however, it is the exception to the rule.

The Alpha Female will come into season once a year only and once mated will be pregnant (gestation period) for around 63 days. During this time she will prepare a small den to give birth in and will enrol one of the middle ranks to act as a nanny to the cubs once they are born so that she can resume hunting duties sooner rather than later but I'm getting ahead of myself – she hasn't given birth yet!

She will give birth to a litter of between four and six cubs, all weighing about a pound each and all born blind and deaf. At around two weeks old their eyes and ears open and they become more active; during this time the mum won't have left the litter for very long, only nipping out to toilet and to collect the meat that the rest of the pack have regurgitated for her.

At around three weeks old the cubs are strong enough to venture out of the den and get their first taste of the big outdoors; they'll hang around the den area for the next month or so with their mum. Once they reach ten weeks they're fully weaned from mum and are being fed from the pack which they instigate by licking at their mouths when the pack return from the hunt – the canine communication signal from a lowly rank to a more senior rank to regurgitate food and look after them (thank goodness regurgitation was one trait that died along the route to domestication).

Leaving the den area for short periods of time to investigate, the young cubs become familiar with the surrounding areas and can join the pack on a hunt at around six months old when physically, they are almost the same size as an adult. Once they are sexually mature at between two and three years old, they either settle into pack life with their parents and litter mates, or move on to join other packs in the area or to set up a pack of their own.

Thoroughly Modern Millie...

In the realm of the modern dog, the *Canis lupus familiaris,* however, you don't have to be a senior rank to have the privilege of passing on your genes – unfortunately, thanks to breeding for looks and unscrupulous breeders you don't even have to be a particularly good specimen...

Dogs are bred for lots of reasons; to improve upon the line hopefully being the top and most important one, however, a lot of the time it's for money or that the owner of a much loved bitch wants 'the same again'.

It's a sad fact that the bitches that are being used for breeding aren't always the best suited to the act or even health checked, however, I've covered this already and don't want to go getting up on my soap box about it...

The pack hierarchy/ranking system is very much alive in pet dogs as anyone who has more than one dog knows. Like the wolf pack it tends to be quite fixed at the top and bottom with a bit of fluidity in the middle. Bringing in a new pack member will cause changes to the ranking system due to the dominance level of the new member against the current pack which is why it's easier, more often, to bring in a puppy (which will naturally work its way up the ranks) rather than an adult dog (whose rank is established and will generate instant rank changes as it asserts itself accordingly).

The other thing that may change the ranking system to an established pack is one of the females being mated. When Bart's breeder Jill decided to mate his half sister Gertie, I decided to keep a log of the pack dynamics before and after the puppies were born so that I could share it and you could get a feel of how important the ranking system, leadership, dominance and subservience is to our pet gundogs.

Sorry if it reads a bit like a soap drama although I suppose that's kind of what is... Jill was down to five bitches when she decided to breed from Gertie, a healthy mid ranking labrador (although the highest ranking of the intact females). Out of the five bitches, the most dominant and the most senior ranking, Fidgit was the only one that lived indoors. She would demand to go first when out and about and would 'block' the other bitches from Jill, always wanting to be the closest. When picking up on a shoot however, Fidgit sits out in front and watches the action ahead of everyone else.

When it came to letting the others out of the kennels, Fidgit would always 'mount' Libby (Beta rank) and would then 'check out' each of the girls as they left their kennels, they in turn would defer to her 'inspection' keeping still and dropping their heads. When returning to the kennels Fidgit wouldn't necessarily go in first but she cast her eyes over each dog as they passed her. Other than mounting Libby, Fidgit didn't pay any particular attention to any one dog. Gertie, along with the other girls, always showed deference to Fidgit... are you still with me? There's a table soon to make it easier to understand...

Once Gertie was mated and started to show her pregnancy at around five to six weeks (a dog is pregnant for 9 weeks) Fidgit started to stand back and allow Gertie to go first showing her deference; Gertie took it and just walked on by as if Fidgit didn't exist. None of the other girls barged Gertie or mobbed her to play from about this time.

Once the puppies were born, Gertie was treated with immense respect and deference by all of the girls (yes, including Fidgit) who would all dip their heads subserviently in her presence; this was at its peak in the first couple of weeks post whelping (giving birth).

When the puppies were three to four weeks old Gertie started to become one of the girls again, investigating rabbit holes and generally being in the same area as them rather than keeping an aloof distance. The more time Gertie spent away from the puppies, the more she became 'one of the girls' again and her status diminished from Alpha Female to second rank.

Pack Dynamics before, during and after Gertie's puppies: born 17th August 2010

Pre-puppies	During pregnancy	Post puppies (November)	January 2012
Fidgit *(spayed)*	Gertie	Fidgit	Fidgit
Libby *(spayed)*	Fidgit	Gertie	Gertie
Willow *(spayed)*	Libby	Libby	Willow
Gertie	Willow	Willow	Inca
Inca	Inca	Inca	Myrtle *(Gertie's pup)*
			Bibi
			Libby
			Mika *(new dog in over the last month, about to move to mid-rank)*

So back to the *Canis lupus familiaris* breeding pair... the breeder decides which of her pack she's going to breed and spends some considerable time choosing a suitable mate, one that ticks all the boxes in relation to temperament, health, the type of puppy that he 'throws' (produces) and of course, looks. She'll present her bitch for mating at around day 11 of the oestrus cycle or she may have the stud dog stay with her for a couple of days. Once the mating has deemed to be successful then no more matings will take place and life gets on pretty much as normal, although care is taken with the newly bred bitch for the next week or so.

Some breeders will get the bitch scanned to confirm for puppies and some wait and see what occurs. In a kennel environment the bitch will be housed in a special birthing kennel, in a home environment a birthing area somewhere in the home is set up, a quiet place away from the bustle of family life. If left to her own devices the heavily pregnant female will head for the bottom of a wardrobe or cupboard, under beds or desks... it's sounding very much like a den that the Alpha Female looks for, isn't it?

At around 9 weeks, or 63 days, the bitch will give birth (whelp) to her puppies, the size of the litter varies drastically from one (singleton) to upwards of 13, although no breeder ever wants either of these extremes as it's too hard on the bitch – a comfortable litter size for the new mum is around six.

Once born the new mum will clean them extensively, not only so that they're clean of any birth residue but also to ensure they recognise her saliva scent; she also licks her nipples regularly not only to clean them but so that the puppies can find them easier as they are drawn to the smell of the saliva.

Birth and Beyond

Puppies are born deaf and blind; they also have very little touch sensation from the shoulders down for a few days as the nervous system isn't completely formed – it is for this reason that tail docking and dew claw removal must happen swiftly following birth when pain sensitivity is at its lowest.

The newborn pup cannot toilet on his own as the sphincter muscles aren't working at this point, instead mum needs to lick the genital area to stimulate the production of waste which she will then eat in order to keep the den clean (this is why the eating of poo is such a natural behaviour in the canine world, natural but totally yucky to us).

The newborn puppy cannot move very much at all as the muscles aren't being fired up by the incomplete nervous system and they have absolutely no substance to them; the best that a newborn puppy can do is shuffle ever so slowly using his head in a pendulum like movement to locate his mum and his litter mates which he relies on for warmth as he cannot control his own body temperature at this early stage. If the pup shuffles too far away from the litter or the litter shuffles too far away from him he may become distressed and mum will either bodily pick him up in her mouth, as opposed to by the scruff, or will flip him over with her nose pushing him into the bundle of fluff that is his siblings.

The puppy is however born with a fully working nose, all 220 million scent receptors are fired up within a few days of being born; the nose really does define the dog's world...

As you might guess the puppies don't really do much at first other than sleep, eat and grow. To me these newborn puppies look just like little moles, especially when they're coloured black and tan.

After around ten to fifteen days, just as the puppy goes into the transition period, the eyes begin to open; it's also around this time that the ear flaps start to lift and sounds, albeit quite muffled, are starting to be heard.

The Transition period: weeks two and three
These two weeks are such an important time for the little puppy. Not only is he starting to see and hear but he's also starting to feel. His temperature is starting to be able to regulate itself which means he'll be starting to move away from the litter to prevent overheating; just as well his front legs are starting to work as he'll be able to drag himself into his own space... More often than not going backwards at this early stage; he'll also start to sit as he pushes his front end up leaving his rear behind.

It's towards the end of this period that the eyes open fully although it won't be until weeks four to six that they can more or less see what an adult dog sees, and it will be another week or so after that, before the eyes start to change from a milky blue towards the colour that they will be as an adult.

The ears also fully open around this time although in pricked ear breeds it will be a couple of months before the pinna is strong enough to stand up. As with the eyes the hearing won't be as defined as an adult dogs until around four to six weeks and then it will take another couple of months for the puppy to learn to be discerning.

The Socialisation period: weeks three/four to twelve
The socialisation period is also known as the 'critical period in your puppy's growth'. It stretches from weeks three/four to week twelve of your puppy's life, and as you might guess from the name that has been given to it, it's all about socialisation.

There is an overlap between the transition period and the socialisation period which is known as the awareness period or the period of awareness and is from days 21 to 28. The change in sensory awareness happens very quickly for the puppy, more or less overnight, and that is when the puppy becomes aware of his surroundings, his mum and his litter mates; it's also a time when he needs his litter and the familiar surroundings the most. As you can imagine this is the worst possible time for him to be taken away from the litter or for the litter as a group to be moved.

The socialisation period is, apart from the period of awareness, split into two distinct learning phases; the first is about socialisation with their own species and learning all about how to be a dog, the second phase is about socialisation beyond their species... that means us.

Canine Socialisation
Between three and seven weeks the puppy learns all about being a dog and he learns it from his mum and his siblings. Once he has all his communication 'gear' in working order it's time to learn how to communicate; this involves using facial expression as well as body language, ear positioning and tail wags. It really is quite comical to watch five week old puppies strutting their stuff, heads held high, ears flattened whilst their erect little tails are wagging away – all very important stuff as they learn how to communicate through posture and, just as importantly, learn to read it in their litter mates.

As well as learning all the posturing 'stuff' these little puppies have to learn what it feels like to bark at another dog and in turn be barked at; they also have to learn how to bite and in turn be bitten. You'll not believe the noise that comes out of the puppies box from four weeks or so; growls, barks, yips, yaps and screams.

My breeder always has a little camera in the box with them and keeps the monitor with her; sitting having a coffee when there's puppies around is amazing – you just can't take your eyes off the screen watching the little souls interact with each other, playing pounce and chase and bite and "ouch you play too hard"... seeing it in action and watching the behaviours unfold naturally is just fantastic.

It is during this time that the young puppy learns about pack hierarchy and his place within it; oh and he also learns about discipline... discipline from his mum and discipline from his litter mates.

From his siblings he learns to dominate or show deference; to climb over or be climbed upon. He also learns how much pressure he can apply with his little jaw... too much will cause a softer puppy to scream and not play any more whereas too much with a stronger puppy will leave him open to be attacked, thereby learning not only how to play nice but also how to show deference to a senior rank to prevent aggression.

His mum will discipline him either by using a paw to pin him in place or a low growl to let him know he's gone too far, especially when she's starting to wean them off the teat; if he really pushes his luck she may air snap at him although there'll be massive amounts of facial expression first; furrowed brow, hard stare, a wrinkling of the nose as well as a general bristling and freezing of the body... all important lessons in canine communication.

At around week four, or there about, depending on litter size and condition of the mum, the breeder will start to introduce a bit of weaning 'mush' to help supplement mum's milk; this is the beginning of the weaning process and of mum starting to distance herself from her puppies, this is the time when the whelping bitch generally looks at her worst as all of her nutrients have gone into producing milk; no more though, once the breeder starts to help out with a bit of mush, mum will start to be able to put on condition again.

Human Socialisation
Between seven and twelve weeks is when the puppy learns how to interact with people, learning about us in the way that he learned about his litter; how to read our facial expressions, our body language and our energy.

He has to learn about our world; about carpets and lino, TVs and radios, aerosol sprays, hoovers, flushing toilets... the list really is endless and he has to be exposed to it all, however, there is one massive thing that is working against us as we bring our puppy home – the fear impact period which runs from weeks eight to eleven...

The puppy's first reaction to many things at this point can be fear and it's up to us as their leader and protector to make things less scary; that doesn't mean we mollycoddle and soothe our puppies, it just means putting a bit of forethought and common sense into introducing our puppies to something new.

As the puppy will be with you, rather than with his litter for the rest of the phases in his development, the information regarding growth and socialisation will come later in the book (within the training element) to save you having to flip back and forwards to see what you should be doing when – it's all in one place and broken down by age.

Leaving the litter...
The most common time for puppies to leave the litter is between seven and eight weeks; before this time and the puppy will miss out on valuable lessons

from his litter mates on how to behave, especially in relation to biting; three to four weeks after this time and you'll be bringing home a puppy right in the middle of the first fear period which, if he hasn't been socialised effectively during the extra weeks by his breeder, can find it harder to adapt to life with you and yours and can be on the nervy side because of it.

Personally, I like to bring my puppies home between seven and seven and a half weeks, that way I know my puppy has had enough time with his mum and siblings to learn about being a dog and it gives me a couple of days grace to settle him in before the first fear impact period arrives. Bear in mind that each puppy is an individual and so the start and end 'dates', if you like, of each phase in their life is fluid by a few days.

Hopefully after working your way through the early stages of a puppy's development, you'll understand why singleton puppies are such hard work and why I would only recommend them to a very experienced puppy owner.

Likewise why bringing home two puppies from the same litter is such a bad idea; one will always be a more senior rank and discipline the other, and if it's not checked by a strong leader (us) can lead to out and out bullying making both dogs lives miserable in the process.

Leadership in action

From the second that you pick your puppy up you are his leader; initially this is a default position, however, by the time the puppy is between twelve and sixteen weeks the position has to be earned, therefore do yourself, your family and your puppy a favour and start as you mean to go on.

That doesn't mean booming at your puppy or getting cross, rather it means working out how you want your adult dog to behave and start moulding your puppy to fit that picture.

Leadership is about maintaining discipline, and reinforcing these boundaries within our daily routines instils this, however in these early days of puppy ownership you'll draw more upon the guiding and teaching elements of leadership and hopefully, by getting this right, the need for discipline when entering adolescence diminishes.

The perfect puppy. Really?

Is there such a thing? My first puppy Kym was the perfect puppy.

I'd wanted a dog since I was about seven and when my dad relented to me bringing Kym home when I was thirteen I was in absolute heaven. She toilet trained herself, taught herself how to behave around the home as well as sitting when told and coming in from the garden; she brushed herself, cleaned up any mess that she made and didn't leave any hair lying around or bits of half eaten chewsticks... The perfect puppy!

"Yeah, right" I hear you say... She was, but only because my mam was doing everything while I was at school and, if I'm honest, I was completely unaware of any of it – just like with babies, it's much easier if you can hand them over to someone else at the end of a cuddle than to have them with you twenty four hours a day tending to their every need.

The first couple of days

So, you've got your puppy home with you, he's had a wee, what now?

Well, now it's time to sit on the floor and relax. If your puppy comes over to you, invite him into your space, if he's having a little wander around the room that's fine – don't take your eyes off him though and remember to keep the doors closed so he can't wander from room to room.

If he starts to sniff and circle you'll need to get him outside again as they're classic cues that he needs a poo (or a wee); don't make a fuss just carry him outside and pop him on the area that you want to make a toilet place for him. Snuffle the grass back and forwards with your fingers to encourage him to sniff, which will in turn encourage him to toilet.

When your puppy's 'performing' say your toilet word over and over again for the duration. When he's done, give him a little puppy treat then pick him up, praising like mad as you do, pop him in his crate and give him another little puppy treat; do not shut the door at this stage. Congratulations; you've just started toilet training your puppy!

Toilet training

The only way to be successful in your toilet training is to be vigilant.

Your puppy has absolutely no concept at this moment in time what is acceptable to his new pack and what is unacceptable; the only way he is going to learn that is by you being vigilant and consistent in your approach.

Your new puppy will need to toilet after eating, drinking, waking up or playing; any kind of snuffling or sniffing an area or circling and you need to get him straight out and into the garden.

Try to get him to follow you out of the house rather than picking him up as the lifting movement will take away the urge and the more you can get him to toilet outside the more he will want to toilet outside. However, if you see him starting to squat, say "no", pick him up (without waiting for him to finish) and take him to the part of the garden you wish him to use.

Encourage him to use the same space in the garden by walking over to it and showing interest with your hand by 'snuffling' the area, you can also do a sniffing noise; you don't have to get down there, generally just the sound of the sniff combined with the smell coming up from the grass that you're disturbing with your hand will be enough to get your puppy's nose down and sniffing.

When he starts to wee or poo, very quietly repeat the chosen toilet word over and over again (mine are 'hurry up' for a wee and 'finish off' for a poo); think carefully about your toilet words and bear in mind that you'll be saying them in front of different types of company and for up to 15 years... I've had clients use 'empty' 'clean dog' 'go toilet' 'go wee wees' 'go Gordon' and so on.

When he's finished give him a tiny treat then make a game of dashing back indoors to his crate and pop him in it and give him another treat; this will encourage him to get straight back indoors after toileting rather than messing around in the garden...

Once he's used to his crate you can close the door once he's back in, give him a treat through the bars and then let him out, building up the amount of time between getting the treat and opening the door for him so that the norm is to toilet and then come and settle down in his crate; start conditioning the routines now and you'll save yourself a lot of hassle later... just be patient with your puppy while he learns.

In time, if you let your puppy out to toilet and he messes around then bring him back in and pop him in his crate for five minutes or so then back into the garden – remember no toilet then no treat.

Make sure that you always use the same door to the garden for toileting so that your puppy knows which door to head to once he cottons on that he needs to go out to toilet. Once he starts indicating he needs to go by heading to the door you can start adding another command or prompt; mine is "Is it toilet time?" which quickly turns to "toilet time" once they're trained and I want them to go.

What you're doing with this little routine is conditioning a response to a word (in the way that you will with 'sit' later on), however, this is quite special as you're pairing the word with a bodily function (through classical or Pavlovian conditioning) and, once you've conditioned it successfully, just saying your toilet word will make your dog want to go... magic!

In the early days remove access to all water bowls (in or out of the crate) between two and three hours before bedtime, this will give him a chance to empty his tanks before bed and will encourage him to be dry overnight, however, if it's very warm then offer him a little water half an hour before his last toilet break. Once he's dry through the night, which should only take a week or so, then start allowing him a small amount of water in his crate overnight.

For the first couple of weeks you're going to have to go to bed late, around 11pm or midnight, and get up early – very early, about 4am to let puppy out for the toilet; don't worry you can go straight back to bed, especially if you don't make a fuss, do everything with dimmed lights and quiet voices. Add quarter of an hour per night to the time you have to get up and before long your puppy will be going from 10:30-11pm through til 6:30-7am.

The first time I realised just how clever my young Labrador was, was when I was toilet training him. I used this method of getting him straight back into the crate after performing as I can't be doing with hanging around the garden, especially in the wind and the rain (as a mid-summer puppy I was toilet training at the end of Autumn).

Unfortunately I made the mistake of giving him a treat when he got back to his crate for 'trying' to toilet rather than for actually doing the deed. After a few days of taking Ziggy out for a 'dribble' or assuming the 'pose' I took him to my vets and explained the situation to her. Upon finishing the examination and with much mirth, Juliet announced that Ziggy had 'got one over on the boss' and was playing me for a treat... oh very funny Ziggy!

Crate training

Up until the arrival of Ziggy, my puppies were trained to sleep downstairs from the first night; however with Ziggy, I tried something different. After many discussions with my friend and colleague Ross McCarthy I decided to bring Ziggy's crate into my bedroom and have him by the side of the bed for a couple of nights.

It worked ever so well and this is now how I start puppies off, that is if the new owners phone me prior to bringing the puppy home as once the puppy's slept downstairs I tend to leave them be...

Feed your puppy all of his meals in the crate so that he associates it with nice things happening. Invest in a couple of puppy kongs and some Naturediet puppy food; stuff the kongs with the Naturediet and keep them in the fridge, then when you return your puppy back to his crate after toileting after a meal, give him a stuffed kong to help him settle down rather than a 'toileting' treat. Stuff it quite loosely to start off with and remember to reduce his meal allowance by the amount of food used in his kong.

Ziggy settling down with his stuffed kong in the back of my car

As with the toileting routine, after the first day or so start to close the crate door when you put his kong in to help him settle down.

Occasionally add food to your puppies bowl while he's eating so that he associates you approaching his bowl as a good thing. Removing his bowl whilst he's eating doesn't mean you'll be able to remove it when he's an adult; it will just make him wolf his food down when see's you approaching or worse, become protective and guarding of his food.

When your puppy is tired encourage him into the crate with a food treat and help him to settle and sleep in the crate by sitting on the floor by the open door and stroke him until he nods off, then quietly close the door, without locking it. Again after a couple of days you can start locking it when your puppy is asleep and build up the time between him waking up and you opening it to let him out; bear in mind, that certainly in the early days, he'll need to go toilet fairly quickly after waking.

When you lure your puppy into the crate with a treat repeat what will be your command word as you do so... "in your crate", "crate" or "go in your crate" all work well; use a different word for his bed to save confusion and in the early days of crate training the crate should be the only bed available to your puppy.

So once he's allowed in the living room you'll have to decide whether you invest in another crate or take his night time one in with you... the crate in your living room won't be forever, you'll be able to replace it with a bed in a couple of months.

When bedtime comes take your puppy's crate upstairs and put it by the side of your bed, close enough so that you can drape your hand on it if your puppy gets unsettled... try to keep everything calm and quiet and no 'cooing' over him at bedtime – take a matronly approach and you'll do fine.

When you hear your puppy start to stir (properly as opposed to just changing position), get straight up with no fuss and only the dimmest of lights and carry puppy down to the toileting area; as soon as he's done straight back to bed for both of you, giving him the tiniest of tiny treats as you pop him in his crate... you can now ignore him or just let your arm drape across the crate until it's time to get up.

After a couple of nights with your puppy beside you, start edging the crate out of the room and on to the landing; before you know it your puppy will be sleeping quietly and confidently downstairs.

Even the professionals can get it wrong, especially with their own and so a word of warning with the stuffed kongs; please don't make the mistake that I did with Ziggy and give them in the middle of the night to help your puppy settle back down - within a couple of days he was demanding his 4a.m. kong!

Introducing a routine

As with babies, the sooner you can establish a routine the better, however don't go at it regimental style and impose it from day one, rather keep the following in mind and build up to it over a week or so.

Try to aim for a routine that goes something like train, play, feed and then in the crate for an hour or so to sleep off the learning, fun and food; then hanging around with you for an hour or so and then back in the crate for an hour with his snuggle safe and a kong.

Then it is train, play, feed and then in the crate for an hour or so to sleep off the learning, fun and food; then hanging around with you for an hour or so and then back in the crate for an hour with his snuggle safe and a kong.

Then it is train, play, feed and then in the crate for an hour or so... you've got the gist of this haven't you?

Have your puppy out with you for a couple of hours after his dinner then you can have a puppy free half an hour (with your puppy out of the room) before bringing puppy in with you for an hour or so before bed.

It's really important for you as a new puppy owner to have some puppy-free time to just relax... it's also really important for your puppy to be on his own while you're in the house so he doesn't become totally dependent on you – it will also make leaving him home alone much easier.

Remember to pick up the water a couple of hours before bed to give your puppy a chance to 'empty the tanks' before bedtime and no exciting play an hour before bed!

Always train before feeding rather than feeding and then training; your puppy will be keener for the treats if he's hungry, and at this early stage you won't know what really motivates him other than an empty tummy. Once you start walking him then you'll walk him before feeding, not only to follow his natural behaviour but to help avoid any digestion mishaps.

In relation to feeding, please feed the best that you can and that suits your puppy's digestion; whether that is a natural diet or a processed one, the choice really is yours... however, don't feed the cheapest just because it's cheap or the most expensive because it is expensive and therefore must be the best; it doesn't work that way. Do your homework and make an informed decision.

Oh and please forget all about socialisation this week, the best thing you can do for your 7-8 week old puppy is to bond with him, toilet train him, crate train him and let him get used to his new home and garden area; and don't overdo the visitors either – he needs to settle in his new environment.

And then some

So you've made it to the end of the first week – congratulations!

Puppy training begins from the second the breeder puts the puppy into your arms and the house training side of it has already started – now it's time to look at the basic obedience side of your puppy's education.

Starting with the sit, stand, down and the puppy recall, we'll move swiftly on to the helpful 'added extras' that I think all puppies and dogs under the age of four months should learn; however, before we go any further we need to keep some things in mind...

Your behaviour shapes your puppy's behaviour

Although you can't start training your puppy until you bring him home, you're kind of shaping his behaviour from the second you think about getting a puppy and imagining how much fun he's going to be and what he's going to be as an adult dog.

You're mentally figuring out what's going to be acceptable to you and what's not... quite often we romanticise getting a puppy (Lady & The Tramp has a lot to answer for don't you think?) and then fast forward to the trained dog picture with the hard work and frustrations of puppy and adolescent ownership a kind of fuzzy grey area in the middle.

Try to keep in your mind that you're not 'training' your puppy rather that you're educating him on what's acceptable, or not, to your pack and moulding him into the dog you've always dreamed of.

I don't know if you saw 'Walking with dogs: a wonderland special' on BBC2 in October 2012, but there was this lovely moment when they interviewed a man who'd adopted a young girl called Daisy and rescued a Staffordshire bull terrier called Zen; he talked about the importance of boundaries and consequences for both Daisy and Zen and ended by saying "it's what you do when you love someone, give boundaries and consequences...".

The words resonated so much with me as a parent and a dog owner that I thought I would include them here... we owe it to our charges (child or dog) to let them know what's acceptable and what's not, what will disappoint and what will please, what will lead to scolding and what will lead to praise... that way they can relax knowing the way of things and can develop their personalities without fear of getting it wrong.

Enjoy your puppy wanting to be with you and everything being really exciting, from opening the post to loading the washing machine; the more things he see's and explores with you the more he'll want to do it with you rather than on his own.

However, try to think before you act as puppies learn so very quickly; they really are like a little sponge absorbing everything around them.

I can remember when Ziggy was little – he was so glued to my side that I decided to get him to chase falling leaves in order to train a recall and get him coming back to me. Before you think 'what a good idea' let me tell you it wasn't... it was a daft idea, a seriously daft one and it was only when I did the photo shoot with Nick Ridley for this book that I realised. I set Ziggy up for his puppy retrieve, sent him after a toy and just as he left me the wind blew – oh yes, you've guessed it... off he went after the leaf – bad, bad idea!

How learning takes place

Every time we do something, nerve cells in the brain, known as neurons are fired up. They talk to each other in a way similar to passing a baton in a relay race, forming a pathway; a neural pathway. In the same way that passing the baton becomes quicker and more fluid with practice, so too the more an action is repeated the more established the pathway and the quicker and easier the action and reaction, until it eventually becomes an automatic learned response like driving a car or riding a bike for example.

The simplest way to remember the process is to think of it like a field of long grass. The first time you walk across the field may take a while and you'll bend the stalks. Next time you'll make more of an impression and so on. By the time you've walked the same path 20-30 times there'll be a bit of a track and you'll be able to walk it faster. Within a short space of time you'll have an established track that you'll use every time rather than walking across the 'untouched' area.

The same but different
Now imagine that the dirt track that you made across the field earlier is now covered with thick ice. The track is familiar but slippery and so you're being tentative walking under the new conditions – you need to call on more resources, more 'pathways', than normal to do a walk you're familiar with.

This is kind of what happens when you take your puppy to a new location, be that a different room at home or a different place entirely, and ask him to do something that we think is familiar - because the conditions have changed the response to them is different.

This is why it's so important to repeat over and over again anything that is being learned in the same systematic way in various conditions.

Say for example you taught your puppy to 'sit' on carpet... that would have fired up the touch sensors on your puppy's pads in relation to the texture of the substance he's on. You'd then tell your puppy to sit - the pathway (to overly simplify it) would be something like "sit".... on soft squidgy fluffy stuff yet firm but yielding, rifle through commands.... come, down, sit ... ah 'sit' got that one; fire up the body mechanics (muscles) to produce a sit.

If you then 'told' your puppy to sit on wooden decking for example, he may not have made the association with the texture he was feeling in his pads with the body mechanics required for a sit and so may flounder. This is why we train on lots of surfaces and in lots of environments so that 'sit' appears in every pathway regardless of what stimuli is underfoot or around in the environment.

As we increase our dogs 'intelligence' through systematic learning they can make the leap from say wooden decking to polished wooden floors, tightly woven carpets to deep pile etc., and so we don't have to train the action, only give the command; a bit like when we first walk on frozen pavement and frozen dirt tracks... we have to learn to apply the same walking technique to both surfaces in order to be confident while walking on any frozen area.

Socialisation and habituation; been there met them
I've got to say it; I have been looking forward to writing this section so much. Why? Because as dog owners we are obsessed with socialisation and, like

anything else we get obsessed with, tend to worry about it, over think it and overdo it.

Socialisation and habituation are two sides of the same coin and just mean getting your puppy used to something; the former on a social level the latter in relation to places. It doesn't mean that your puppy should be allowed to jump all over people and dogs or go hooning around with all and sundry... neither does it mean that you should let your dog go exploring everything he feels like.

Nope; it's all about being comfortable in new environments, with their own species and with ours. Remember that what you instil now will stay with your puppy for life and that means if you teach good manners and polite behaviour around people and dogs, that is what you'll get when your puppy becomes a fully grown dog. Whilst it might be cute to watch your puppy jump up on your friends or your friend's dog it won't be nice when your puppy is an adult and covered in mud.

I see many, many dogs that as puppies were allowed to mob other dogs, both on and off lead, in puppy training classes and outside, and those dogs are an absolute nightmare. They grow up thinking that it's their right to jump all over other dogs and drag their owners around to say hello, or, if they're not allowed to, will bark or lunge towards the other dogs out of frustration or even turn and bite their owners.

Their owners, out of either embarrassment or through being given poor advice, will holler out "oh he just wants to say hello" meaning that either they know what's going to happen if they try to walk by without the dog getting his own way, or, if the dog's off lead, that they don't have a recall. Hmmm...

Now that doesn't mean that you shouldn't allow your puppy to see other dogs or people, or play with other dogs or people, all it means is that you set the boundaries for the socialisation, say who your puppy can say hello to and who your puppy can go play with.

Hey you look like me

What is really interesting, and hopefully at some point you'll get to witness it yourself as it's fascinating to watch, is that dogs tend to group or socialise by type... type and colour.

On one of the courses that I co-tutor with Ross McCarthy, we let our dogs, along with our assistant tutor Vicky Lawes' dogs, go off lead in the paddock to 'free range' so that our students can observe how the dogs interact with each other and to learn about canine communication. Even when we bring in strange dogs the pattern always repeats itself; the dogs group together by type and by colour, for example the long haired dogs hang out together (Spitz' and Goldie), the German Shepherds hang out together and then those of the same (or similar) colour, the black Labrador and the Rotties.

Dogs know what other dogs look like from their time with mum and their siblings; they also know their colour, or their shade, every time they look at their paws or nibble at an itch; if they live with another dog of a different breed or colour they get that too, however, anything outside of this sphere of knowledge is, as you might guess, alien to them.

One of the girls who trains her Labrador with me also has wirehaired Daschunds and she has noticed this too – the Daschunds are totally oblivious to any dog they see on their walk unless it's another Daschund and then they get 'a bit lively'; funny thing is Angus is the same – he'll happily walk along and ignore any unknown dog unless it's another Goldie then he'll watch them with interest and turn his head to watch them walk away.

Are you a dog? Really?
When my breeder Jill has puppies I try to take Angus down in the week or two before they go to their new homes... not so that the puppies can come up and 'meet him' but so that they are exposed to a large 'flouncy' dog as opposed to the smooth Labrador bitches that they're used to. The puppies will look on from their place of safety in the whelping kennel with the funniest of looks on their faces while they try to figure out what this big bouncy flouncy ghost of a dog is that is frolicking and bounding about.

Being quite a large dog, even for a Golden Retriever, Angus doesn't really come across many dogs that are bigger than him and tends to take everything in his stride; that was until he came across a Great Dane or rather three fully grown Danes and a youngster who was head and shoulders taller than him. It was the first and only time I've ever seen Angus out of his depth around other dogs.

Having such a well balanced and well socialised dog, it didn't enter my head that he would find the Danes intimidating and yet when we went to Ross's and the Danes came over to investigate he looked totally flummoxed and very insecure being towered over and never left my side for the day while I was working... Ziggy however, having been brought up with a big dog was in seventh heaven and spent the day hanging out with all the 'big boys'.

And it's not just size and flounciness that your puppy will need exposure to in time, and note I said "exposure to" not "hoon around with", colour definitely comes into it.

My hubby was walking the dogs for me one morning when he came across three black working cocker spaniels all off lead. One of them came over to say hello and was absolutely fine with Ziggy my black lab, however, when Angus started heading over he turned on Angus... As Ziggy was head and shoulders taller than the little working cocker and as the cockers have a fair bit of fur, I can only presume it was Angus's colour that the little dog hadn't had much exposure to, either that or it had had a previously bad experience with a Golden Retriever.

Do I know you? Are you sure?
And it's not just different shapes, sizes and colours of dogs that you need to socialise (read 'expose') your puppy to – you also need to find different shapes, sizes and colours of humans too... as well as a range of clothing and smells.

Children are the obvious ones in relation to size and also are the ones that we need to take the most care of introducing; we don't want the puppy (or dog) to think that children are fair game to chase or bully, or that the yummy smell of sickly sweet milk and dirty nappy is anything other than completely out of bounds for anything other than a wee sniff.

If you know any people of different colour to you and your family, invite them round to ignore your puppy so your puppy learns how to 'read' them... black people's faces, like black dogs faces, can be very difficult for a dog to read as the light plays across the face in a different way; by learning this art at an early age your puppy will never get worried by meeting black dogs in the street – you will be surprised by how many dogs do and indeed how many black dogs are attacked because of their colour...

Beards, glasses, caps and noisy, smelly, swishy coats all need to be worn around your puppy at some point, although not all in the first couple of days or weeks I hasten to add.

Let your puppy see you put them on and take them off as dogs have no concept of clothes and as far as they're concerned, you sound like you and you smell like you but you've morphed into some sort of alien with massive black eyes and a funny shaped head. If you don't know anyone with a beard then slap some shaving foam on or tie a hankie around your nose and mouth so that your face is partially obscured... sounds daft but it may save your dog from being wary of bearded men or sunglass-wearing, cap-toting folk walking towards them.

Vaccinations.....

Depending upon your breeder, you may be bringing home your 7-8 week old puppy having already had his first vaccination – let's hope not as his immune system will be very immature at this early stage in his development and many vets, my own included, like to wait until they're 9 weeks old before they start their immunisation programme.

Vaccinating your dog, like vaccinating your child, is a very personal and emotive subject and I have friends who vaccinate their dogs and friends who don't; I also have friends that vaccinate until their dog reaches a certain age and then stop, however, the majority of them all agree that regardless of whether you're going vaccinate ongoing or not, the puppy vaccines are a must.

I know you may be reading this and be thinking you should always vaccinate or you may be reading this and be thinking you should never vaccinate and go down the homeopathic or herbal remedy route, however, as a behaviourist all I'm going to say is do your homework, weigh up the pro's and the con's and talk to your breeder and talk to your vet and make an informed decision.

Training your puppy the basics: 8-12 weeks

YES! Training at last!

Now that I've planted some seeds in your mind and given you something to think about over the next couple of weeks in relation to socialisation etc., it's time to get onto the really exciting and wonderfully fulfilling part of training your puppy the basics.

Only teach one exercise per training session which should last, certainly in the first week or two no more than a couple of minutes and repeat throughout the day; I recommend that every time you put the kettle on you have a training session while waiting for it to boil – if you're not a tea or coffee drinker then try to do between eight and ten mini sessions a day, so for example do two on training the sit, two on training the down, two on training the stand and so on...

I always start puppy training using treats, my favourite being the ones that Natures Menu do; they're 95% meat, smell yummy, aren't full of junk and can be split quite easily into six or eight little pieces which is perfect as it means you'll only need one treat per training session.

Lastly, before we really do get on to training, you need to think about a release command for your puppy – I say "OK" along with a ruffle on the top of the head to mean that they're free to move or I just give them another command, for example I would heel them out of a sit stay. To release them from my side when out on a walk I say "Off you go, go play".

A word of warning about the 'OK' release command; a couple of years ago I had young Ziggy out with me at a class and the dogs were in a sit stay. I said to my handlers to leave their dogs and walk around them in a circle and was amazed that Ziggy got up; replaying it in my mind I realised that what I actually said to my handlers was "OK, leave your dogs and..." It has caught me out a couple of times but to be perfectly honest I haven't thought of a better release word.

The first week, or two

Over the next week or so you should be looking to train your puppy how to sit, stand, down, come when called and to walk loosely alongside you... don't panic and think it's a big list, remember your puppy is a sponge and the more you can play this game called training the easier life will be when you hit adolescence.

This first week is all about introducing the concept of training (for you and your puppy) and so the exercises that you train will be in their most basic form with your puppy being in front you. Please don't rush it and try to get your puppy to do the exercises on the move or by your side this week as we'll be extending the exercises at the appropriate time, however, please read ahead as it will give you a good idea of what you'll be aiming for and when.

Try to use a quiet voice when training your puppy... if you train your puppy using a booming sergeant major voice you'll always have to use a booming sergeant major voice. No, much better to train commands using a calm, quiet voice then, if you ever have to use your lungs to get your puppy's attention, then oh boy will you get his attention.

Remember this week is all about bonding with your puppy, letting him settle in his new home and introducing the basics in order to occupy and satisfy your puppies thirst to learn new things, which over the next couple of months is at the highest it will ever be... stay calm, think 'educate and mould' rather than 'obedience training' and don't lose your temper or get angry with your puppy.

Sit

Teaching your puppy to sit is one of the most important things you'll ever do; if, once it's taught, you don't want your puppy to do something you just say sit and his bottom goes down interrupting any behaviour that you want to stop.

You can train this little exercise quite informally by just scooping your puppy's hind end towards you with one hand while the other steadies him at the front end and popping him in a sit, in the early days he'll be almost sitting on your hand; say very quietly "sit" as you do so and stroke him in that position.

To more formally train him to sit take a piece of treat and take it to his nose; this is to get his nose working for you and to get him really interested in what you're doing, then take it above his head and, in an up and over movement, slowly take

the food towards his hindquarters. As he puts his backside down on the ground say "sit", tell him what a good boy he is and give him the treat.

If you find he starts walking backwards then slow down your movement; whereas if he tries to jump up lower your hand as you've raised it up too high too soon and remember it's the action of sitting that gets the treat so no giving him the sweetie (dog treat) until his bum is down!

Once you've got your co-ordination sorted out you may want to start holding the treat between your index finger and thumb in a 'pincer' grip with the rest of your fingers straight.

This will help prepare your puppy for the sit/stop/stay hand signal which you'll use later - when you stop training with food in a month or so, all you'll need to do is straighten out your index finger and you have a conditioned hand signal, similar to that used by a policeman to stop traffic, or, in our case, our gundog!

A note for all the spaniel owners reading this... spaniel folk tend to use the word 'hup' to mean sit so if you're thinking of taking your gundog out with other spaniel folk then you may want to replace 'sit' with 'hup'.

I've never really got to the bottom of where this word came from in relation to telling a dog to sit, however, I have my own little theory... I reckon it came from those naughty spaniels not sitting properly when told to do so – the owner (and I can see a weathered old beater in a flat cap as I'm writing this) probably said something like "will you up sit up, come on hup!"

Down

Teaching the down is such a valuable exercise to train your puppy, and although it's not traditionally trained in the world of the gundog, in the world of the pet dog it is a must. It will make teaching your dog to settle down or go on his bed much, much easier and hopefully will mean you'll be invited back to friends' homes with your dog.

Put a couple of tiny treats in your hand and let your puppy know that you have them. Lure him into the down by slowly placing your hand between/in front of your puppy's front legs. Keep your hand on the floor and give your puppy a second or two to figure out what he's meant to do.

Using a treat lure your puppy into a down position

If he bows and stays in the bow position fold him into a down with the other hand by gently pushing on his raised backend - push away from you rather than straight down. If he doesn't lie down and doesn't bow then put the heel of your hand on his shoulder blades with your fingertips towards his backend and fold him down as above.

When he's in the down position, release the treats as you remove your hand and say "down". Always reward your puppy for downing by putting the treats on the floor rather than from your hand as this will (hopefully) keep him in the down position as you remove your hand rather than popping out of the position as soon as you move.

Stand

Teaching the stand is another one of the fundamentals of puppy training; in the months and years to come you will be so glad you invested some time in training this little exercise.

Why? Well it's great for when you're grooming, drying off after a wet walk or much later, doing a stay in filthy weather whilst you're clambering through a fence, however, for me the most important reason for training the stand is for your visits to the vet.

Your vet cannot get the thermometer where it needs to go if your dog is sitting, and it's pretty awkward when the dog is in a down – for this to happen easily and without stress for all concerned your dog should be standing... and I mean standing, not shuffling forward; the last thing you want is for your puppy to shuffle off the table or, later, be part of a comedy skit where he's walking in a circle around you whilst your vet is following along behind trying to hang on to a thermometer... 'stand' equals 'stand still'.

Before you train the stand though you must have trained either the sit or the down as your puppy must be in one of these positions to start with. So, put your puppy in either a sit or a down and give them a little treat or simply praise them; turn to face your puppy and very slowly lure him forward with a treat until he stands.

Once he's standing let him nibble on the treat and say "stand", "good boy, stand"; if he sits or lies down, just lure him forward again.

The puppy recall
There is absolutely nothing formal about first teaching your puppy to come... all you want to do this week is make yourself more interesting and appealing than anything else; if you've brought your puppy home the way suggested earlier, you'll be more or less there already.

When your puppy is looking in your general direction, make a silly noise and pat your legs; as your puppy starts coming towards you give him a big beaming smile and say his name followed by "come". When he's with you give him a sweetie, a cuddle or play with him.

If he gets a bit over-excited with playing then keep it low key by giving him a stroke and a little sweetie instead.

Walking to heel
Although I've called this walking to heel, in this first week it's about getting your puppy to want to be with you as you walk around the house. When your puppy is with you, slowly turn away from him, patting your left leg as you do so and to encourage him to come with you, praise with a "good boy" and after a few paces bend down and give him a stroke and a treat if you feel inclined.

When my puppies are this young, I tend to say things like "come on then", or "this way" followed by their name rather than using the "heel" word... plenty of time for that; all we want is for your puppy to feel comfortable hanging around with you and being reasonably close to your leg.

Before we get too far into the training - have you thought about which side you want your adult dog to walk on?

If you're right handed then your dog should really walk on your left, if you're left handed then your dog should walk on your right. Why? Well it goes back to when the dogs were used as war dogs, armoured up and on the battle field. The soldiers would have their sword in their right hand (or left) and their dog on the opposite side, under their shield arm. Nowadays when we shoot, a right-handed 'gun' will have their dog on the left and vice versa.

Although this is not set in stone, as they say, it does make sense and is a good maxim to follow...

Putting on the collar

At some point during the first week you're going to have to put on your puppy's collar. Put it on with no fuss and take a matronly approach. Once it's on give him a treat and let him get on with it... by this I mean, shaking, scratching or rolling.

Once he's settled with his collar on, take it off, give him a treat and then put it back on and leave it on. The collar should be a proper puppy collar, very light and unadorned (baubles, beads and fancy bits can get caught up) and you should be able to put two fingers under it; check the fit every second day as you'll be amazed at how quickly your puppy grows and the last thing you want is a tight collar on his little neck.

The first month

Presuming that you got your puppy at 8 weeks, by the time you finish this little (or not so little) section, your puppy will be 12 weeks old or 3 months.

Don't go for perfection on one exercise before starting the next one, rather aim to introduce your puppy to all of them during different training sessions, improving the response each time.

Little and often is the key and will see the greatest improvement in your puppy, prevent your puppy from getting bored and save you masses of frustration.

And please don't feel overwhelmed by all of the exercises in this section – it's designed to give you enough to occupy your little sponge for four weeks which is a long time in the world of the puppy. The gundog is one of the more 'intelligent' of the breed groups; they really do pick things up extremely quickly and have an unbelievable thirst to please you in these next couple of months so exploit it to the max and get all the basics in now while you are your puppy's God.

Extending the basics
Sit

Once you have your puppy sitting nicely in front of you it's time to start teaching him to sit at your side as well.

While your puppy's sitting use a little treat to keep him in place (but only let him sniff it at the minute) then turn yourself so that your puppy is positioned by your left leg, take a baby step forward encouraging your puppy to come with you by luring him with the food and after he's moved a pace or two, slide the treat up your leg, his nose will follow and say "sit" – he's got the concept that sit means 'put bottom on the ground' and so his backside will go down.

The trick with keeping your puppy in the correct position by your left leg is to keep your hand level with the seam of your jeans, or where the seam would be, that way your puppy won't get too far ahead of you... to make it easier you can put the side of your thumb on your leg to prevent you swinging your arm around and luring your puppy forward which is a really common mistake that we all do when learning how to train a dog.

Down

Once you're past the first week and you've been teaching the down then you can start to stand up while your puppy is still in the down position.

Do as you have been to get your puppy to lie down, then as you go to stand up put another couple of treats on the floor between his front paws; this will keep him in the down position as you get up – remember to say "down" when your puppy is in 'the down'.

Stand

When your puppy is happily standing still and nibbling on the treat in your hand it's time to start fiddling with him, bearing in mind this exercise is for grooming, drying and for the vet to do their 'bits'.

Slowly, calmly and gently start to stroke your puppy with your free hand; if he tries to move away keep your hand still rather than removing it as all that will teach him is if he moves away from your hand you'll stop. Stroke the full length of his back and introduce stroking his ears, stroking his legs, lifting his paws, stroking his tail and putting your flat hand between his hind legs.

Remember this will take a month or so to introduce so don't make it a mammoth desensitisation session - it will take time.

Come and sit

Over the next week or so when you play your recall game, start to withhold the treat until your puppy is sitting in front of you, however, don't say "sit" as he comes in, rather use the treat as a lure to pop him into a sit, as you did last week in the initial training of the command.

Now when you say "come" what you mean, and what you're teaching, is that "come" means come and sit nicely in front of me.

Another recall game is to stand in front of your puppy with both of your hands in front of you holding a treat between them and start to shuffle backward luring your puppy with you and say "come" as you do so; after a couple of shuffles, stop and lure your puppy into a sitting position and give him the treat when his backside is on the ground.

Walking to heel

I always start to train my puppies to walk to heel before I even think about putting the lead on; I want my puppy to think that the best place in the whole wide world is by my left leg and it's much easier to do that without the distraction of a piece of nylon dangling down from me to them.

Take a treat in your left hand and position yourself so that your puppy is on your left; it doesn't matter what position your puppy is in to start off with. Put the treat up to your puppy's nose and walk a couple of 'baby' paces luring your puppy with you and then feed him; remember to keep your hand on or by, but not in front of, your jean seam as described earlier in the sit... you will have to

As your puppy gets the gist of it, stand up and reward intermittently

bend down so remember to take lots of breaks not only for your puppy's sake but for your back's sake too.

Now is the time to introduce the word heel as you're walking by just saying "heel, good boy... heel". Remember to take it slowly though as he's still very much a baby.

Repeat the above until you and your puppy can comfortably do about 10 baby paces interspersed with sweeties, then start withholding the treat for a couple of paces; just turn the back of your hand toward your puppy so that your hand stays in the same position but your puppy cannot get the food as it's facing to the front, then turn your hand back towards your puppy and reward. Over the next couple of days you can start to play with this little routine by turning your hand away and back a couple of times without actually feeding your puppy.

Build up so that you're doing about ten paces without feeding your puppy then feed your puppy, lure him into a sit and reward him and end the session.

Once you can do about ten paces without feeding you can also start to stand up, instead of turning your hand away stand up instead, then to keep your puppy interested and keen, bend down and give him a sniff of the treat before you stand up again... remember the bigger the puppy the less you have to bend – you may even get away with leaning sideways or doing a bit of a side bend which is better for both you and your puppy as your face will be further away from him thereby encouraging him not to jump up.

If he tries to jump up it's likely to be because you have your treat too high for him to reach comfortably but low enough for him to think he can snatch it out of your hand by jumping at you – either bring the treat down to his nose or move it higher up out of temptation's way.

If he gets ahead of you turn slowly away from him and walk the other way, patting your left leg and saying his name to get his attention along with the 'come on then' command that you were using initially; once he's walked to heel for a couple of strides give him a treat.

Go to heel; a.k.a. 'The Finish'

This is a little exercise that makes it easy to move your puppy round from sitting in front of you to sitting at your side and in time will become part of your recall but for now it's trained as an exercise on its own. In the early days of training it, try not to do the finish immediately after your puppy recall as the clever puppies will cotton on that one follows the other and will start putting themselves to heel before you ask and before you're ready for them; instead, when training the recall, just turn away from your puppy when he's sitting in front or put yourself into the heel position without him moving.

Put your puppy in a sit facing you; try to start early on to position yourself and your puppy squarely to each other and quite close so the tips of your toes are facing, and almost touching, the tips of your puppy's paws.

With a treat in your left hand lure your puppy out to your left hand side as you move your left leg slightly back out of the way keeping your right leg still. As your puppy moves say "go to heel", "good boy go to heel".

As your puppy gets behind you draw him in and forwards as you put your left foot back to where it was originally – it will look as if your puppy has just done a little anti-clockwise circle to get to your left leg.

Using your treat, lure your puppy into a sit by your left leg and give him the sweetie...

Whistle conditioning

For the next couple of weeks you're going to start conditioning your puppy to the sound of the whistle. Any whistle will do providing it's not silent as I want you to be confident that your puppy has heard it rather than blasting away on it. My preference is the Acme gundog whistle 211½ as I find the 210½ too shrill... The numbers refer to the pitch and tone, the ½ at the end meaning that there isn't a pea in it (like the thunderer referee whistle) and are often referred to as 'eleven and a half' or 'ten and a half'.

I can remember ordering my first lot of gundog equipment over the phone years ago – it was in the days of internet infancy and the shop was found using good old Yellow Pages. After giving the man my list of goodies over the phone he repeated it back to me giving the whistle its full name of two eleven and a half... "no, I only want one" was my reply; how he contained himself enough between his smothered sniggering to explain the terminology to me I'll never know. Just as well I have a sense of humour and can laugh at myself as there have been many such blonde moments over the years!

So, once you have your whistle you need to decide what your recall is going to sound like – mine is peep-peep peep-peep, a soft double peep done twice; the first double peep gets my dogs attention and gets them turning towards me, the second brings them home. The only sound that is reserved in gundog terms is a single pip which means sit, but there's plenty of time for that later.

Please practice with your whistle away from your puppy so that you can make the same sound over and over again as you're going to condition your puppy to it and need to be consistent... and please bear in mind that your puppy has fantastic hearing and so you can blow quite softly, especially softly as part of this little routine.

For the next couple of weeks, just as you put your puppy's food down for him to eat, softly blow your chosen recall whistle.

Holding the collar and treat

At various points during the day gently take hold of your puppy's collar and encourage him to you while you're holding it and give him a treat; likewise once he's happy with the various positions of sit, stand and down hold his collar when he's in these positions and give him a treat.

Why? Well you want him to think that you holding his collar is a really good thing, whether that's escorting him to his bed when he's older or putting his lead on after playtime, you don't want him ducking out and avoiding your hand.

Also, if your puppy is concentrating on the hand that isn't going to be holding the collar, then he's less likely to bite and chew at the hand that is!

Getting the lead on

At some point you're going to have to introduce your puppy to the lead. Most puppies will try to chew it or bite at it... if this is the case for your puppy, cover the lead with bitter apple spray (see chewing things below) and try again; if he's insistent then train the leave it! command for a couple of days and then try again applying the 'leave it!' if necessary, however, if you leave introducing the lead until this stage in your training, that is after you've taught your puppy to walk nicely beside you as well as sit etc., then you shouldn't have a problem.

Pop your puppy in a sit in front of you and reward (at this early stage it can be a food treat but in time a 'good boy' with a smile will suffice), attach the lead while he's sitting, tell him what a good boy he is and give him another little sweetie. Leaving your puppy sitting, pop yourself into the heel position and lure him forward a pace or two saying "heel" as you do so... after a couple of paces pop him in a sit, take the lead off and have a play with him or give him a treat.

Do this a couple of times going no more than a couple of paces before taking off the lead; give it a couple of days before embarking on training loose lead walking.

Loose lead walking

When your puppy can quite happily stay with you to heel for 10 or so paces and is happy having his lead on for a couple of paces, it's time to start loose lead walking puppy style. Now nothing changes, not your position, your puppy's position or the position of your treat; all you're going to do is put the lead on your puppy and hold it in your right hand leaving it loose between you so that it's not straight, rather it's a curve or slightly looped, hence the term loose lead walking.

Exactly as you would without the lead, take a treat in your left hand and position yourself so that your puppy is on your left. Put the treat up to your puppy's nose and walk a couple of 'baby' paces luring your puppy with you and then feed him; remembering to keep your hand on or by, but not in front of, your jean seam. You

It's not the end of the world if your puppy jumps up; just take a breath, keep going and try to keep your 'treat' hand tucked in

can pick up where you got to walking off lead with loose lead walking.

If your puppy gets ahead of you turn and walk the other way, patting your left leg and saying his name, rewarding after a couple of strides and if he scoots or tries to scoot around behind you, just ever so gently guide him back into the correct position as you walk, remembering to praise him once he's in the right place.

Teaching your puppy to settle on his bed

The easiest way to teach your puppy to settle down on his bed is, in the early days, just sitting on the floor and having a cuddle.

If you've invested in a dog bed as well as your crate then put the bed beside you as you sit on the floor. Use a treat to lure your puppy onto his bed and as you do so say "on your bed" or "in your bed" whatever rolls off the tongue for you, however, don't give him the reward until you've lured him or helped him into the down position so that the command means go and lie down on your bed rather than just putting a paw on it!

If you haven't invested in a bed yet, and in all honesty I don't blame you as there's going to be a lot of teething going on in the next couple of months, then use a bit of vet bed instead; the good thing about using vet bed to start with is that it's easy to take to friends houses, your puppy recognises it as a 'place to rest' from his crate and when you do go for the posh bed you can place a bit of vet bed on it first to help keep it clean and to transfer the command to a new 'thing'.

In time you'll start to edge the bed from by your side to the position in the room that you want it to be in and encourage your puppy away from you and into their bed, helping to keep them on it with a stuffed kong or a dog biscuit; as you build up your 'stay' training you'll be able to increase the amount of time your puppy stays on his bed as he'll become confident being away from your side... then 'on your bed' will mean go and lie down on your bed and stay there until I say you can get off.

Introducing the stay

Okay, 'stay' sounds a bit grander than it really is... all you're doing to start off with is pausing prior to rewarding your puppy, whether that is in the sit, stand, down positions or on his bed.

After you've paused a few times and your puppy holds the position then say "stay" and reward – there's no point in introducing the 'stay' command if your puppy is moving around or squirming as all you're doing is conditioning the word 'stay' with 'squirm'.

When you can pause and use the 'stay' word then say "stay", lean your shoulders slightly away from your puppy so that you're putting a little bit of distance between your faces, say "stay" again and then go back to your original position and reward and release.

Aim for your puppy to be able to stay in one position for about five seconds by the end of this section, that is, when he's twelve weeks.

Grooming
From the second you bring your puppy home you're getting him used to being touched by people, normally on the head or around the ears or maybe a tummy tickle, however, that's not enough to desensitise him to the touch and make grooming a pleasant experience for you both.

When you're sitting on the floor with your puppy, either beside you or in the early days on your lap, make a point of stroking your puppy all over – the full length of his back, his legs and paws, his ears, his tail and not forgetting to occasionally include his 'bits'. Do it calmly and quietly with no fuss - as if 'this is the way it is'... your puppy should start to enjoy the attention, especially if you do it when he's tired and looking for some 'cuddly' time.

By the end of the first week you should be 'fiddling and faffing' most nights (but not every time you cuddle your puppy) and should also be looking to include running your fingers over his nails.

Once your puppy is happy with the attention on your lap and you have taught him to stand, then you need to start fiddling and faffing with him in the standing position, but not enough to get him moving around.

Whenever you pick up a paw say "paw", when you gently look at his teeth say "teeth", when you open his mouth say "open", when you look in his ear say "ear" – you're getting the hang of this, aren't you?... it means when you do go to the vets and they have to look in his ear it's not a big deal to your puppy – you say "ear" and he knows what's going to happen next.

Use this time, and later, when you're grooming your dog, to check for lumps and bumps and burrs and ticks, as well as, of course, bonding with your dog.

My dogs line up to be groomed when my husband picks up the brushes, more so than with me as I tend to do it in a perfunctory manner while they're standing whereas my husband lets them lie in the sitting room and takes his time brushing them... and they absolutely love it; they love the feel of the brush (which helps improve blood circulation to the skin as it gently massages it) and they love the attention that comes with it... Angus, my Goldie, is normally sound asleep and snoring by the time he's finished. Do take the time out now with your puppy to condition them to enjoy the fuss and attention that grooming brings with it.

For the first month you could probably get by with a baby's hair brush or a very soft bristle brush just to get your puppy used to the sensation of being brushed; go softly and slowly but in a matronly fashion and if your puppy squirms or starts to make a fuss, use a treat to help focus his mind and when he's relaxed being brushed end the session, even if you've only brushed his right shoulder three times – you can do the left one tomorrow; all you're trying to do at the minute is make the brush a pleasant experience.

Check with your breeder, or your vet when you get you puppy health checked, the best kind of brush to use for his type of coat and when to start introducing it.

Working with a line

House lines are shorter, thinner, lighter versions of the long line and are a great investment when you get your puppy. Once you've trained your puppy to accept the lead and not chew it you can use your house line in the garden to restrict your puppy to a toilet area if they're inclined to go off exploring; you don't always have to hold it, just let him drag it around – it's very light.

The lines are also great for when you visit friends and you're not sure that their garden is puppy proof or to keep your puppy near you when you're in their home.

I love them, and as they're only about two and half metres long, I tend to use one as a lead as it means you can easily go from training walking on a loose lead, to the recall game of walking backwards and saying come without worrying about running out of lead length.

Playtime!

Playing games is an intrinsic part of your puppy's makeup and while in the litter will spend a lot of his time playing with his siblings. As you now know this 'play' is about the puppy learning the skills that will ensure he stays alive and at the rank that he feels he ought to be at.

Playing on their own with toys is about taking some of their energy away, learning how to wrestle things to the ground as well as stalking and pouncing; toys help with teething and they're fun boredom breakers.

When we play with our puppy it's important to have ground rules as the last thing we want is for him to play the stalking, pouncing, attacking game with us, more so when there are children in the house.

Playing with puppy should be kept calm, no rough housing or encouraging the puppy to bite or scrabble at us and no playing pull with a toy, until the adult teeth are in, as you run the risk of pinging out baby teeth or misaligning his jaw if you pull hard to the side. If your puppy keeps trying to incite you into a game of pull or tug, then put the toy on the ground and hold it there with your hand so that your puppy can pull without you pulling back as that is when the damage is done.

Without getting overly technical about it, a dog's jaw, unlike ours, never fuses at the chin to make it one solid bone, rather the two sides knit together on a bit of cartilage called the mandibular symphysis, a bit like how our pelvis goes together at the front. Like the front of the pelvis (pubic symphysis) opening when women give birth, so too can trauma cause the manibular symphysis to move out of alignment; this does get a bit more robust as the dog matures (although a mandibular symphyseal fracture is not uncommon), but as a puppy it is less so and is something that I'm always quite precious about – especially for a gundog where we never want their mouths to be an issue for them.

Games of chase, even with a little puppy, should be banned from day one; you and I both know that at some point you're not going to be able to catch him, either that's because he's faster than you or can get under the table where you can't get to him... at that point you have quite successfully communicated to your puppy that he can't be caught if he doesn't want to be which really doesn't bode well for your recall training.

Games of 'fetch' and 'catch', both favourites of mine, are covered in 'Bringing out the best in your gundog puppy' later in the book.

Good Manners around the home...

Just as with young children, it's really important to instil good manners in your puppy. Do so as a matter of course throughout your puppy's day rather than making a 'training' exercise of it, before you know it your puppy will be minding his own manners and will be a joy to be around. And, when you get to take him round to your friends it will a lot less stressful for you, your friends and your puppy.

Feeding time

Once you've trained a sit and your puppy knows that to get the treat his bottom needs to go on the floor, exploit the association before you put his dinner down for him, whether that's a stuffed kong or a bowl of food.

The key is not to tell him to sit, just to hold the food in front of you so he has to look up; when he sits put the food down for him...if he goes to get up just lift it up again but not so high so that as soon as he sits you can put it down.

Before you know it you'll have the food down and your puppy sitting. To start off with, as soon as the food is down, give your puppy his release command so that he knows it's okay to eat, however try to build it up so that you can put food down and then pause before you release him.

Don't start this until you've finished the two weeks of whistle conditioning at mealtimes... not so much for your puppy but to save any confusion in your mind as to what we're doing, when and why.

Furniture or floor?

This is for you to decide... but, and it's a big but... how would you feel in a year's time when your puppy is no longer cute and cuddly but is instead more or less a fully grown dog; he gets into the sitting room straight after his wet muddy walk having rolled in some fox poo on the way back and jumps straight up onto the settee or on Aunt Flo who is sitting having an afternoon nap?

If you don't want your adult dog on the furniture then don't let your puppy up... it really is not good for his joints to be clambering up and then jumping down and, providing you're vigilant in relation to keeping an eye on your puppy, there's no reason why he should ever push his luck when he's older and try getting on the settee or armchair.

If however, he does get up then just unceremoniously remove him, saying 'no' as you do so; no treats or fuss for getting off as otherwise it will either turn into a game of chase or your puppy will learn that the easiest way to get a sweetie is to jump onto the settee.

Sit for attention

Once you've trained your puppy to sit there's absolutely no excuse for your puppy not to sit for attention. If your puppy comes over for some attention, lure him into a sit, just as if you have a sweetie in your hand, and then stroke him when his backside is down, alternatively, while he's still very young, scoop his backside under him until he is sitting.

If he gets up while you're stroking him remove your hands and say something like "ah ah" and encourage him back to a sit – remember no stroking unless his backside is down, then regardless of where you are, he knows the only way to get any attention is to sit.

Make sure the rest of your family and your guests follow this little rule as well. Similarly, once your puppy is a bit older and going out with you, make it a rule that people may only stroke him when he's sitting.

Doors and doorways

These two things hold so much interest for puppies (and for grown up dogs too for that matter) as there's always something happening on the other side... the saying 'the grass is always greener on the other side of the fence' springs to mind.

At this young age it's all about exploring and the excitement of getting out of the door and to somewhere new. As your little puppy grows, however, there will also be an element of competition over who gets out of the door first as the first out will get to the toy on the other side or get to go play in the garden first... it is in this area of the doorway that puppies really can learn to barge and more importantly from their perspective, that they can barge into you and then you just step back and let them go first: not the best demonstration of leadership I'm sure you'll agree.

While your puppy is very young position yourself between your puppy and the door using the outside of your leg, sorry, 'silently' using the outside of your leg to gently guide them away from the door as you slowly open it. If your puppy goes to move forward use your leg to push him back again; when you can open it without your puppy moving forward, and it's safe to do so, then you can either let your puppy go through first or can go through calling your puppy with you as you go.

When your puppy is bit older, around twelve weeks, you can start closing the door in front of your puppy, however, if you've been doing the above since he was nine or ten weeks then you probably won't need to do this.

Quite simply as you go to open the door, instead of opening it fully just open it an inch or so and then close it with a resounding snap, again you'll do this without saying anything. Repeat a couple of times until your puppy is backing off... you're aiming as you move into the next chapter of the book to be able to stand with a door open and your puppy not wanting to go through it without permission.

Please be careful with the old wooden style doors that have 'lips' on them and don't practice this technique on them at all. Puppies are incredibly quick and you can catch a little paw between the threshold and the lip causing damage... practice the routine on other doors; I've found that it's easier to start with doors opening away from you.

Remember to use this little routine of opening a tiny bit and then shutting the door with a snap to teach your puppy not to barge out of his crate when you open the door; good manners, even at a very early age, are absolutely essential.

And, although it should go without saying, I'm going to say it anyway; practice doorway manners after you've got a good idea of your puppy's toilet routine and once your puppy can hold his bladder a little otherwise you'll either cause a toilet accident or make the 'urge' go away and cause an accident later.

Knock, Knock
This is a really good routine to practice with friends and family so that you gain confidence prior to having to deal with the situation for real; you could have

them read this section so that they know what's expected of them to make life a little bit easier for you.

In the early days, whether you're going to the door for the postman or to bring people in, please leave your puppy in his crate or, if he's not in it when the door goes, then put him in it.

If you're worried about taking too long to answer the door then put a little notice up to say that you're puppy training so may take a little longer than usual; bear in mind many postmen and delivery men get bit or live in fear of being bit and so will be absolutely cool with waiting an extra minute or two and will probably appreciate you making the effort to train your puppy.

Once your puppy is happy on the lead, so hopefully around the 11-12 week mark, then you'll take him with you to the door. Invest in two or three spare leads and have one hanging on the back of the door where your crate is, one on the back of the kitchen door and another by the front door.

When the door goes encourage your puppy to come with you to the nearest lead, pop him in a sit and put his lead on then, using a treat, have him walk to heel to the door and sit when you get there. Open the door, beam a smile at the person waiting and say that you're puppy training; remember every time your puppy goes to get up put him in a sit.

When you've finished dealing with the person at the door and the door is closed, give your puppy a treat, release him and take his lead off.

You can always have a bowl of wrapped sweets to offer your postman or delivery person while you're working at puppy training; it will give them something to do and take a bit of pressure off you as you desperately try to keep your puppy's backside on the ground.

A word of warning when dealing with people at the door; do not let them stroke your puppy or give him a treat... once he's trained then it's your choice but initially I would advise against it.

Why? Think back to socialisation – it's about your puppy being comfortable and relaxed in a situation: if all and sundry who come to your door make a fuss and feed your puppy he's not going to find it very relaxing – he's going to end up positively bouncing and totally over-excited about going to answer the door with you.

Nope; you want people coming to your door to be a boring every day event that your puppy can take or leave.

Come in...
When you answer the door to invite people into your home, go through the same routine as if it's the postman. Once your puppy is sitting nicely by your side, invite your guests in (reminding them to ignore the puppy for the time being) and using a treat, walk your puppy to heel into whichever room you and your guests are going to be in.

Keeping your puppy on lead either sit yourself down and stand on the lead, or prop yourself up against a kitchen bench and stand on the lead... it's now everyone's job to ignore the puppy until he relaxes, when he does so you can very quietly take your foot off the lead. If he gets over excited or tries to jump all over your guests just take the lead again and pop him into a sit, give him a reward and stand on the lead again.

Remind your guests that they can stroke the puppy as much as they like providing he's sitting and his front feet are down... the playing rules also apply to your guests as well as your family.

When you have people around and your puppy isn't quite comfortable being on a lead, very quietly let him out of his crate, toilet if need be and then ignore him until he relaxes – if he's jumping up at your guests then show them how to scoop him into a sitting position and quietly stroke him.

The more you teach him good manners around your family and friends the greater joy (and less stress) you will receive in return.

Leave it!
This has got to be one the favourite exercises that I teach, not only for new puppy owners but for new dog trainers that attend the Professional Instructor Skills workshop that I co-tutor. It is really easy to teach, the puppies (and dogs) pick it up incredibly quickly and it is such a valuable thing to train.

Always train this little exercise away from all of the other things you're doing with your puppy at the minute as you'll be training him to turn his head away from food.

Hold a small to tiny treat in a pinch grip between your thumb and middle finger keeping your index finger tucked in. Offer your puppy the treat and gently say "Good, take it". Do this at least five times.

Then offer your puppy the treat and do not say anything. When he goes to take the treat, lift up your index finger and gently tap the side of his nose with it saying "leave it" as you do so. As soon as your puppy turns away from the treat, regardless of how slight, a pause or hesitation counts, then give it to him with a "good, take it". Do this another couple of times and call it a day for this session.

By saying "good" followed by "take it" you're giving your puppy permission to take the treat from your hand. If you make a habit of saying this whenever you hand feed your puppy (training the sit, down etc., excepted), in a very short space of time your puppy won't take food from someone's hand without permission to do so.

Ziggy always used to leap sideways when I gave the hand signal and said "leave it"

In what feels like no time at all you'll have a hand signal of a raised index finger coupled with saying 'leave it' to turn your puppy's nose away from things; give it a little bit longer and you'll be able to use either command or hand signal with great effect.

NO!

Until you've conditioned the word, 'no' has absolutely no meaning whatsoever to your puppy.

As a child we learn what 'no' means from our parents as they use it along with a negative consequence, either removing us from something or something from us, then as we get older they may reason us out of doing something but generally it's a case of "no, don't do that" or "no, don't do that because...."

Unfortunately your puppy has absolutely no concept of reasoning and neither will your adult dog. The part of the brain that deals with reasoning and starts to develop in us when we're about three years old doesn't, and never will, exist in the canine brain. This is why we have to be absolutely consistent with what we tell our dogs to do and why we have to be very black and white with no shades of grey.

To condition your puppy to the word 'no', quite simply the first time he does something that you don't want him to do, make a bit of a drama about it; slap the bench or drop a heavy book and say "NO!" very loudly.

Your puppy will more than likely look to you, and you will be watching with a look of outrage and disgust on your face... turn on your heel and walk to the other side of the room.

Give it a second or two and call your puppy over, scoop him into a sit (if he doesn't look as if he's going to on his own) and calmly give him a stroke... misdemeanour forgotten.

Safety first

Keeping your little puppy safe is one of the most important things you're going to be doing over the next couple of months; sounds obvious I know, but I've lost count of the amount of puppies that I've seen who are allowed to charge up and down stairs and are left to their own devices in the garden for an hour or so at a time.

Vigilance really is the key with a little puppy, actually it is the key with any dog but especially those under around 8 months old as that is the time they're more likely to turn into escape artists and get into mischief, however, even when your puppy becomes a fully grown adult dog, mentally you have to compare him with a toddler... and you wouldn't leave your toddler in the garden or roaming around the forest for hours on end.

Travelling by car

Please don't let your puppy jump in or out of the car; pick him up and put him in the crate and vice versa. For safety's sake, or rather for joint's sake, please assist the spaniels until they're about 8-10 months old and the larger breeds (labs, pointers, spinones etc.,) until they're well over a year.

As noted earlier, keep your puppy safe by using a crate either in the back if you have a hatchback, an estate or a 4x4 or on the back seat; when he's a bit older and beyond the chewing and destroying stage then a dog guard or a harness will work just as well.

Please don't let your puppy be loose in the car, apart from that first journey home... not only will he be a major distraction but you'd never forgive yourself if you had a crash and your puppy was killed or worse killed one of the passengers as he hit them at speed; it doesn't bear thinking about but it could happen if your puppy (or dog) is not secure.

Oh and never let your puppy have his head hanging out of the window... not something you're likely to do with a small 12 week old baby, but bear it in mind for when he's a bit older; having his head out of the window could result in him losing an eye if he gets something in it at speed or he could inhale a nasty or, if you forget he's there, you could hit him with a lamp post or anything you get a little bit too close to.

Stairs & steps

Although I've already covered steps and stairs as part of preparing your home for your puppy's arrival, I thought I'd mention it again here; not just for your puppy's safety but for yours too.

The last thing you want when you're walking downstairs is to have a puppy under your feet, or puppy toys that have been left by a puppy playing on the stairs or for the carpet to be loose from little puppy teeth pulling away at it.

Keep yourself and your puppy safe and ban them from the stairs until they're a year old and then instil good manners so that they don't try to barge past you, in a similar way to how you did with doors and doorways.

Help!

It would be nigh on impossible to cover all the things that new puppy owners need help with, however, the main things that I've found are getting the puppy to settle down, which if you follow the advice above shouldn't be a problem; then there's jumping up, mouthing and chewing. These three things are what drive most puppy owners to distraction as not only do they hurt but they can put children off dogs for life if they're on the receiving end, so...

Jumping up

The only way to combat a young puppy's jumping up is to train a good sit and be really consistent on not stroking your puppy until he is doing so. If he does jump up ever so quietly just put his front paws on the ground and pop him in a sit position.

Avoid bending down over your puppy and having your face low and towards him as it may encourage him to jump up as he tries to greet you by licking at your mouth as he would with a senior rank; instead, try to go down on your haunches (rather than kneeling) keeping your face away from your puppy's and be prepared to prevent him from licking you as this is the contact he wants - if he gets it by jumping up he'll be getting rewarded for doing so and will try again and again.

Things like scarves and dangling earrings are best avoided at this time as well as fancy cuffs and flouncy hemlines.

Mouthing

Mouthing is, unfortunately, part of bringing home a puppy as it was part of his repertoire of communication with his litter and something that 'he needs to go through'.

He needs to learn how much pressure to put through his bottom jaw when using his mouth; whether that is on a toy to make it squeak or on a chewy to bring relief to his teething... and of course, how much pressure on us is acceptable behaviour or unacceptable behaviour, in the same way he learned it in his litter.

It's not something that can be avoided or something to get angry or exasperated about... it's just something that every single puppy owner has to go through.

So, when you first bring your puppy home and you feel his little teeth on you, shriek and I mean **SHRIEK** as loud and as high pitched as you can (in general rather than leaning towards him) and get up and walk away from your puppy with a look of absolute disgust on your face. Just like his litter mates would do, you've said to your puppy that he plays too rough and you're not interested in being with him.

It is really important that you don't stay near him and I can't stress enough how important it is not to laugh, especially when you see the comical look on his face.

Give it a minute or so and then make yourself available for a cuddle again, however, if puppy does it again then make sure you repeat the procedure and giving him a longer time out.

If it continues then put him in his crate for a time out in there, and no, he won't associate the crate with being a bad place; that only happens if you shout and scream at him as you put him in it.

If you have children then you can put some Gannicks bitter apple spray on the cuffs of their jerseys and also their socks and hem lines but apply it away from the puppy so he doesn't see it happening and flood his senses with it as detailed below first.

Chewing things

Chewing and puppies go hand in hand I'm afraid, or rather furniture and teeth.

I can remember when Bart was a puppy and we went out for dinner leaving him with our friends son who was babysitting for us. I went through all the puppy stuff with him before we went out... all that is apart from, yup, you've guessed it, chewing.

We returned from a lovely night out to find that our furniture had been well and truly crimped by sharp little puppy teeth. Luckily he hadn't taken any chunks out, just left perfect little teeth marks all the way round an ottoman and a table.

Another instance of chewing, again with Bart, was once when I nipped upstairs to have a shower without putting him in his crate. When I got back downstairs he'd chewed his way through the plaster in the hall to the point where you could make out the colour of the breeze block, however, wood was Bart's thing, as it is with most labradors, and he did manage to get through an architrave and two skirting boards on the two other occasions that I forgot to crate him before going out.

Remember your puppy has no concept of posh wood, to him wood is wood is wood and that lovely polished table leg will probably be just as nice to chew as the manky old stick in the garden.

Do yourself a massive favour and don't let him chew sticks when in the garden or anywhere else for that matter; not only will it give him a taste for wood but he could also end up with splinters in his mouth, get the stick jammed on the roof of his mouth or perforate organs if he swallows it... sticks and dogs, contrary to popular belief, do not belong together.

Gannicks Bitter Apple Spray

This bitter apple spray is my favourite deterrent for chewing and mouthing. Citronella spray is also good but it means we have to walk around smelling of citronella whereas we can't smell the bitter apple; also I like to keep the citronella spray for later, when a young dog takes it into his head that jumping up may just be fun, normally around four or five months old.

This is the bit that I hate but it works so well and makes the bitter apple such a powerful ally in your fight against mouthing and chewing. Take some kitchen roll and saturate it with bitter apple spray. Very quietly and without speaking or smiling or anything remotely reassuring, gently hold your puppy and put the kitchen roll over his nose – he will try to pull back from it or wriggle as to him it smells vile. Keep it there for about five seconds then remove it and use it to wipe down table legs or wall corners before popping it in the bin and washing your hands.

Then pick up one of your puppy's toys and have a little play, or a cuddle; it's key to act as if nothing is wrong as you don't want your puppy to be wary of you whereas if you baby them at this stage you'll be affirming that there's something to be worried about and you'll be praising his hesitancy.

When your puppy is not around spray the bottom of all your furniture, especially table and chair legs, corners of skirting boards and anything that you think may be appealing for a puppy.

Forget that you ever conditioned your puppy to the bitter apple and your puppy will too, that is until he tries to chew one of the treated areas and then yuck!

The first fear period

Your puppy's first fear period or fear impact period as it's more commonly, or technically known, occurs between weeks eight and eleven, just as you're bringing your puppy home. Anything that is traumatic or scary or sometimes just big, bold and noisy can have a lasting effect, however it doesn't have to.

Let's just say for example a tray falls on the floor and your puppy scoots off down the hall... your first reaction may be to baby him "there there baby, it's just a tray falling on the floor, nothing to worry about" and you may carry him back and give him a cuddle.

Alternatively, it might look so funny that you can't help but laugh, even as you're going towards him to reassure him that it's okay.

Alternatively, you could do nothing other than walk over to the tray pick it up and carry on doing what you were doing.

The last one is the way to react; the first two are praising the reaction, in this case fear, confirming that when your puppy hears a loud and unexpected noise the correct response should be fear and running away. Remember you cannot reason with a puppy, or with a dog, and reassurance, cooing over and fussing all count as praise in your dogs eyes and when does your dog get praised? When he's doing the right thing.

It is also during this time that your puppy will visit the vets for his welcome home health check and, if you're vaccinating, then for his first vaccination. Try to make them separate visits so that the first time your puppy gets to go to the vets it's a nice experience for him, so that he associates the smell of disinfectant with sweeties and good things happening.

Ziggy, my youngster, is the only dog I've ever had that has been worried by the vets; he's a very, very soft dog and although he didn't flinch when he was microchipped he never forgot and it took almost two years for him to take a treat from vet.

With the new legislation that is coming in with relation to microchipping it means that puppies will be going home already microchipped which means you won't have, or have had, a say as to when the microchipping takes place; the only good thing is that it is before the first fear period so it won't have quite such a dramatic impact on the softie dogs.

And the not so basic: 12-16 weeks

At around twelve to thirteen weeks your puppy will be moving into another stage of his development which will last until he is sixteen weeks of age and moving out of puppyhood and into adolescence.

This is called the Seniority Classification period and is all about your puppy learning about leadership and where he fits within the pack, what the boundaries are, what he can get away with and what he can't.

It doesn't happen overnight, rather it's a build up over four or five weeks and for the majority of puppy owners it's a time of frustration; they feel as if their cuddly little ball of fluff is deliberately doing something to 'wind them up', whether that's running away from them in the garden or chewing anything and everything the second their backs are turned.

They're really not; just like with a child about to start, or having just started school, your puppy is checking the boundaries and testing that they still hold true now that he's starting to 'grow up'.

Your puppy is going to go through some serious changes physically as well; you'll probably notice that at times he doesn't look quite so level at the shoulder and the back end as the growth spurts tend to make puppy grow back end, front end, back end, front end and at some point in the front end growing the baby teeth start to get pushed out and some serious teething occurs.

Now is the time to invest in some hard plastic teething toys, keep them in the fridge so that they're nice and cooling to your puppy's hot gums and make sure you always leave one in the crate for him to give him some relief when he needs it.

If you're into homeopathic remedies then Nelson's Teetha, designed for teething children can help your puppy through this stage if it bothers him; like with children losing their baby teeth some go through with no discomfort whereas with others it's a bit of a painful drawn out process.

Not surprisingly, this period of growth is also known as The Age of Cutting and is not only the time that the puppy cuts his adult teeth, but also the time of cutting the apron strings!

Getting the leadership right now will save you a monumental headache in a couple of week's time...

Training your puppy, keeping him focused on you and taking control of all of the situations that you find yourself in with your puppy, all contribute to great leadership skills.

Remember you're moulding your puppy into the dog of your dreams, a dog that is obedient, fun to be around and that hangs on to your every word.

By making training fun, but keeping the discipline there, will get you all of these things and more... so, remember to smile when your puppy is getting it correct or trying his best and frown when he's getting it wrong rather than when you're concentrating; if he does something that you particularly don't like show shock and disgust which will help to bring him up short (imagine stepping in cold, squishy, smelly dog poo in your bare feet while you're half asleep – yup, that's the face to use).

By bringing in facial expressions this early on in your training you'll make it easier later... I tend to raise my eyebrows and look surprised for example when a puppy tries to snatch things from me; once he's put together the facial expression with an unacceptable action on his part, all I have to do is raise my eyebrows to stop puppy in his tracks – raised eyebrows in my house means that I mean business!

It also means that your dog is watching your face for visual cues just as he would with another dog, making him much more responsive to your wishes.

If you want to explore facial expressions, and I would suggest that you do as it really does help not only with dog training but with life in general, then look at Paul Ekman's work (his website is under useful contacts at the back of this book).

Training exercises for your puppy

Now that your puppy is twelve weeks old no doubt you're itching to get out and about with him and show him off, so apart from improving what you've already done with your puppy, this section is all about getting out and about and meeting other dogs and people.

This is also the time when you'll be looking to start puppy classes a.k.a. puppy socialisation classes a.k.a. (but please not) puppy parties. If you do decide that this is something that you'd like to do then please, please heed all that was said earlier about letting puppies mob each other. There is such a massive variation of puppy size and age at puppy classes and the last thing you want is for your little puppy to feel intimidated and scared of big puppies or for your big puppy to turn into a bully.

If you do go to classes and you feel uncomfortable with what the instructor wants you to do you can always politely decline to do an exercise or an activity; any instructor worth their salt will understand and not push the issue and remember your puppy is your puppy; you get to say what he does and does not do... not anyone else.

How to get really cool heelwork

By the time you get to twelve weeks hopefully you will have your puppy walking to heel and rewarding maybe every ten to twenty strides; time to stretch your puppy a bit now and introduce some changes of direction.

About Turn!

To start off with we're going to do some right turns and some left turns. When you make a turn, regardless of whether it's left, right or about, shorten your strides so that you're almost shuffling; not only will it give your puppy a 'heads' up as to the fact that something is happening, but when you turn away from your puppy he's going to have to work twice as hard to keep up.

Bear in mind that my dogs walk on my left so my left turn has me turning across the front of my dog whereas the right turn has me turning away.

As you think about turning, slow down, encourage your puppy to your leg and say "heel"; as you turn to the right bend down slightly and smile at your puppy and say "heel" again and once you're on the straight stand up, go another stride or two and give him a treat. Go another couple of paces and repeat the exercise so you're in effect working your way around a right hand square.

When you do your left turn, slow down, put your left hand to your left leg and encourage your puppy to your leg as you turn; you can have your food reward in your left hand if you like to start off with so that you're not tripping over your puppy as you first make the turn... in a very short space of time you can forget the food lure.

The reason for bending down on the right turn is to encourage your puppy to keep up, and by smiling at him you're being engaging, interesting and motivating him to come with you.

The reason for not bending down on the left turn is that you're going to be turning towards your puppy, so moving your face closer to him and which could, if you remember, encourage him to jump up.

When you are confident that your puppy can do right and left turns and continue on for ten paces or so of heelwork after the turn before needing a food reward then it's time to introduce the about turn.

An about turn, in either direction, is quite simply two turns done one after the other; I know, I know, it's obvious but, when you're trying to train a puppy, coordinate him, your feet, your hands and a food treat you kind of forget.

Your puppy is still very much a puppy at this point in his education so for now, these are training exercises which teach your puppy how to hold his position by your side rather than as a way of enforcing your leadership (which is one use of a left turn for an adult dog and is discussed later).

Forward march!
Well marching is over-stating it slightly... a shuffle jog slower than a normal walking pace is more accurate!

Once your puppy is quite happily pootling alongside you for food rewards every ten paces or so it's time to vary not only the speed that you're going to go but also when you give treats; sometimes after five paces, sometimes after fifteen, or if you have a good position twenty... remember to use your voice and your facial expression to keep your puppy with you.

By the time your puppy is sixteen weeks you should be looking to vary the speed that you walk, sometimes walking very slowly and sometimes speeding up to a shuffling jog – the key though is to keep your puppy in the correct position.

Hitting reverse
Yup, you've got it... try at some point to heel your puppy backwards, only one stride at a time to begin with. This will only happen if you're upbeat with your puppy and he's focused on you; if you're not upbeat and making it a game then he'll probably just sit.

And these little turns and changes of speed and direction will turn loose lead walking into a bit of game where your puppy (and at this stage he is still very much a puppy) thinks it's fab to be with you as you're so interesting he just never knows what you're going to do next.

The name of this game is instilling leadership... you lead and he follows. Think of it as a dance where you know the steps and your puppy doesn't – you have to guide and encourage him not only to keep step with you but to allow himself to be led.

Much easier with a herd animal like a horse, harder with a predator, as if a predator follows the wrong leader, or a leader who isn't strong enough to lead them then the pack may not eat and therefore not survive; with a herd animal it's not such a big issue as all they have to do is put their head down and food awaits them.

Watch me!
Just like with most exercises that we train our puppy, there are many ways to teach your puppy to watch you, however, this one I developed a few years ago especially for my gundog folk as sometimes we want our dogs to be totally focused on us but without using food or going "watch me" in a high and grating voice.

You will need your lanyard on as we're going to condition your puppy to look at your face when you hold your lanyard.

You don't need to put your puppy in any particular position but he needs to be in front of you to start off with. Put your left hand (remember I'm right handed) in your pocket to get it out of your way and put a treat in your right.

Let your puppy know you have food by either opening your hand and letting him see it, or by letting him have a smell, then bring your hand up hold to your lanyard. Once your hand is on your lanyard keep it still – no waving your whistle around.

Initially all you're looking for is for your puppy to look up at you and then you reward him. When you can count to five with your puppy looking up at you while you hold your lanyard it's time to start talking to him... in a boring, dull, unanimated way, without saying his name and without saying "watch me". If he looks away at any point remind him of the food, hold on to your lanyard for a second or two and then reward... it just means you've gone a bit far a bit fast or you've added distraction too soon.

When your puppy can sit and gaze at you for a minute while you talk in a monotonous monologue it's time to introduce the exercise with your puppy sitting to heel; remember to reduce the amount of time you expect your puppy to focus on you initially as you've made the exercise more difficult for him.

Once you've taught this you can use it when you need attention, for example when you meet people in the street, when you meet a rowdy dog and want your dog's focus (and I put dog's focus not puppy's as by the time you've conditioned this sufficiently to use when a rowdy dog is around your puppy will definitely be a dog).

Sit, down, stay or should that be wait?
Up until a few years ago there was no such thing as 'stay' or 'wait' in the gundog world; 'sit' covered all the bases. This is great when you have an outdoor dog, which is what the majority of gundog trainers train, however, when you're training an indoor dog, a pet, then you need an extra command... one for you as opposed to all and sundry who come visit your home.

Just imagine when your puppy gets older and that your son's mates come round. They hang out in the kitchen chatting away and tell your dog to 'sit' and then wander upstairs to play on the latest xbox game – all thoughts of pooch sitting in the kitchen out of their mind. At some point your pup is going to get up and go for a mooch around and at that point he'll learn that 'sit' doesn't mean 'sit until I tell you move', it means 'sit until you're bored or a smell gets your attention or...'

Nope – keep the 'stay' and the 'wait' commands for yourself!

So when to use 'stay' and when to use 'wait'? Well I use 'stay' to mean 'stay in that position, be it sit, stand or down, until I come back to you and tell you that you can move' whereas I use 'wait' to mean 'wait there, there's another command coming' and so use it prior to recalling or retrieving or if I want to go somewhere first (for example over a fence) and then want my dog to follow afterwards.

Training the stay

Once you're able to put a bit of distance between yours and your puppy's face by leaning away at the shoulder and your puppy stays put for ten seconds, it's time to start moving away from him.

It's always easier to start with a sit-stay as sit is the first exercise we teach our puppy and will therefore be the most conditioned, although if you have a really good down then you may want to start with that position, however, I wouldn't recommend you start with stand as it's too easy for your puppy to move from, whereas the sit and down positions require a bit of effort on their part to get up and follow.

I'd also recommend that you started your stay training on lead as, if your puppy does move, it's easier to prevent them running off and inciting that favourite of all canine games 'chase'.

Have your puppy sitting to heel and, as you have been, lean your body away from him only this time as you give the 'stay' hand signal (which is in effect, the sit hand signal but coupled with the word stay) say "stay" and take a step to the side, but leaving the closest foot beside your puppy giving him confidence not to get up and come with you.

Build the time up to five seconds or so over a few sessions and then instead of returning to your puppy, repeat your stay command take your left foot out to join your right so that you're standing a full stride away from puppy; repeat the stay command and return to your puppy, hesitating for a couple of seconds before you give him a stroke and tell him what a good boy he is.

You can, when your puppy is ready, add another sideways step and when you can do this it's time to start stepping out in front, however, it's important not to rush this as the reason for starting to go to the side is so that your puppy doesn't feel abandoned and to get him being confident sitting away from your leg – if you stride off as you leave him he may feel unsure and try to follow you.

When your puppy is happy and confident with you taking a couple of paces to the side for three or more seconds then it's time to step to the front. Give him the 'stay' command, take a step forward, about turn and come straight back to your puppy's side.

As with stepping to the side build up the time that you are away from your puppy; duration first and then distance so building up to maybe twenty seconds one pace away from your puppy (and facing him) before taking it up to two paces.

Bear in mind that whenever you increase the complexity of an exercise you must decrease it in another way so for the stay, when you take that second pace away (increasing the complexity) you must reduce the time in the stay (decreasing the complexity) otherwise you are setting your puppy up to fail.

Training the wait
I tend to train the wait in a really informal and fun way, starting with playing the retrieving game or a game of catch (see 'Bringing out the best in your gundog puppy') and then transfer it to the formal recall so we'll be covering 'wait' later but I wanted to mention it here for completeness.

Out and about
So far all of the training has taken place in the home or in the garden, however, now your puppy is able to go out it's time to introduce some outdoor training.

Please don't be disheartened the first time you take your puppy out if you feel as if all of your training has gone out of the window; it has but it hasn't. In the same way that we have to learn to walk on packed snow or sheet ice the first time we experience it, so too does your puppy have to learn how to sit on different surfaces; add to that the sights, sounds, and, most importantly, smells and it's amazing that your puppy doesn't spontaneously combust.

Bear in mind that your puppy has 220 million scent receptors in his nose, is very close to the ground where the smells will be most concentrated and he can smell not only what is there now but potentially what was there last month as well...

If you've always restricted your training to the back garden then please do some training out the front before you go into the big wide world as it will be an easier introduction, however, if you don't have a front garden then it's time to start hanging around outside your front door and watch the world go by.

Sitting on your step with your puppy in front of you, or beside you is a good way to start, that way he'll draw on your relaxed state and be able to take it all in while being still rather than rushing through all the smells.

When you're ready, aim to do five or ten paces of good heelwork, plus a couple of sits and then back indoors; that coupled with standing still and chilling out for a few minutes really is enough for your training session outdoors. Try to do this three or four times a day, building up the distance that you go – don't aim to go round the block the first time out!

If you start this when your puppy is twelve weeks old by the time he's sixteen weeks you'll feel as if you're 'walking the dog', however, walking or not – at this stage it's all about training and loose leads, not going out for a social gathering with friends; save that treat for later - much later.

How much exercise

This one is probably going to surprise you if not shock you... puppies need very little physical exercise; mental stimulation yes, physical exercise no.

I'm always horrified when I get phone calls from puppy people that have been exercising the energy out of their puppy; one of the worst was a fourteen week old working cocker that was being taken out for walks lasting over an hour, all off lead... I just wanted to put my head in my hands and cry – the poor wee thing must have been exhausted and aching all over... plus it bode badly for the owners then training it to walk nicely on lead and come when called.

It was just another of those many incidents that made me to decide to write The Pet Gundog series.

The general rule of thumb that relates to exercising puppies is that you add five minutes for every month that the puppy has been walking, so at twelve weeks, or rather three months the exercise level should be no more than ten minutes at a time, so a ten minute walk (although it'll be more like a training session on loose lead walking) twice a day maximum, bearing in mind that this is on top of all your little indoor training sessions.

If you're using this book as a training programme of when to train what, then you should be building up to two fifteen minute 'walks' a day at the end of this section which will take you to four months, but, please don't be rigid.

You're going to be teaching your puppy masses of stuff; basic obedience, good manners around the home, basic gundog work as well as introducing him to the great outdoors; he will be tired and doesn't need endless walking...

When to train... and where

A quick answer to when and where to train is "all the time, everywhere!"

Every time you interact with your puppy you're training him on some level; he is a sponge at the minute, learning about your body language, tone of voice, mannerisms and that's just his natural observation and learning how to communicate with his pack.

There's all the other stuff like when you're tired he can do things that he can't when you're not; when you're on the phone you're fair game as all you do is wave your arms around and pull funny faces; and when the "I don't mind him jumping up, I love dogs" brigade are around he can do exactly what he wants, learning that you that won't say no to a stranger.

Every second of every day you are training your puppy, whether you realise it or not; teach good manners as a matter of course, and for me, that also includes walking on a loose lead at all times.

Going for a coffee

From around twelve weeks I encourage puppy owners to get out and about with their puppies, a little sooner if possible.

Now that's not going against vets advice of not letting puppies out before their second vaccination as I advise, rather strongly, not to put the puppy on the ground...

Find a nice outdoor cafe that you and your puppy can go to and while away a bit of time at. We have a fab one in my local town, and I would sit with puppy Ziggy all bundled up in a towel on my lap and watch people, and the traffic go by, and, providing people asked first, then he would get lots of strokes as well.

As your puppy gets a little older, is used to the lead and knows 'sit' then park as close as you can to the cafe and do the same routine that you did when leaving your home for the first time; stand by your car until your puppy relaxes (allowing no one at this point to stroke him... all that will do is incite excitement and make the next trip harder) and then get your food treat and encourage your puppy to walk to heel to the cafe; there is no rush to get there, take your time and insist on a loose lead.

When you get there pop him on a towel and either give him a stuffed kong and tell him to settle down/go on his bed or get him to sit or lie nicely beside you; when he's settled you can then use your leaders prerogative to decide who can and who can't stroke your 'sitting' puppy.

Meeting a friend's dog

Meeting a new dog is always intimidating and so best done in your own home if possible. Have your friend bring their well behaved dog (you really don't want to introduce your young puppy to badly behaved dogs) around to yours and leave your puppy in his crate.

When everything is nice and calm and your friend's dog is in a down stay then let your puppy out of the crate; keep the dog in a down position if you can whilst your puppy investigates and then put the dog into a sit; before you know it the puppy will be doing his own thing.

Please don't let them bound around and play as not only do you risk your puppy being hurt but you're teaching him that when a dog comes into your home 'all bets are off' and it's playtime.

Teaching your puppy to do nothing

You want your puppy to think that hanging around with you is the best thing in the world; when you're on the move he wants to be too, when you're doing nothing he wants to be too.

Just in the way that you sat on the step with your puppy and stood at the car then so too you're going to get into the habit of doing nothing out on your walks... and it is one of the hardest things in dog training to get into the habit of; when you're on a walk you want to be walking, when you're training you want to be training, not hanging around doing nothing, however, there are times, many times, when you're out and about and doing exactly that... meeting friends in the street, browsing a shop window, having lunch in the pub or waiting your turn to do an exercise in a training group.

Stand still for a minute and watch the world go by... if your puppy starts to wander off, take a little step away from him and give him a gentle prod with a finger; when he comes back to you smile and continue admiring the view – if the prod isn't enough say his name in a fast and almost, but not quite, sharp way as you do so. He'll get the hang of it very quickly and the more you do it the easier it will be for your puppy to just chill out when you stop and do nothing.

Feeding the ducks

Never miss an opportunity to train your puppy. If something excites him then take some time out, there and then, to desensitise him to it; it will reap vast rewards as your puppy matures.

I used to take Ziggy down to feed the ducks when he was a puppy because I wanted him calm around birds that were moving as I knew when I got him that I would be working him on a shoot at some point.

From around fourteen weeks I would drive to the car park alongside the river and heel him along the river bank, stopping regularly I'd put him in a sit and feed the ducks; a biscuit for Ziggy a biscuit for the ducks, a biscuit for Ziggy a biscuit for the ducks and so on, ensuring that he stayed in a sit regardless of what was happening... because there were more treats forthcoming he sat totally focussed on me and would only really look at the ducks when they came out of the river and up beside us.

Training a recall

You've already been training the recall around the house and in the garden, encouraging your puppy to come and sit in front of you. Now we're going to up the ante slightly and teach him to come to heel when you blow your whistle; so make sure you've been conditioning him to the sound of your recall whistle at feeding time and training the 'go to heel/finish' for at least two weeks before you start this.

When you're in the garden with your puppy and he's mooching around, either on or off his houseline, position yourself so that you're facing him with a sweetie in your left hand. Blow your recall whistle and as he looks at you, smile and nod and put your left hand forward and lure him round to your left leg as you did for teaching the 'go to heel'... you're doing exactly the same thing only faster and without him sitting in front first. In time you'll be able to keep your legs still and just lure your puppy round and into the heel position.

Give him a jackpot of treats, which is two or three treats one at a time coupled with a 'good boy' each time.

You can now choose whether you call your puppy with "come" (meaning 'come and sit in front') or use your whistle to bring him straight to heel... remember though to continue training both as they are equally important to your gundog.

whistle your puppy ...

then lure him round ...

... and using a treat guide him into the heel position

Making it formal

When your puppy is happily doing a sit-stay for about ten seconds, you've been using the 'wait' command as part of your retrieving and you've got your puppy coming when called around the home, it's time to introduce a more formal recall.

I tend not to introduce the formal recall too early as I want my puppy to relax in his stays and not expect to be called as soon as I'm any distance away from him, hence leaving it until he's doing a ten second or more sit stay.

Pop your puppy into a sit and, using the sit hand signal say "wait" and leave your puppy in a sit, or rather a sit-wait. Walk two or three paces away from your puppy and turn to face him. Count to two and then tell him to "come". Reward him when he's sitting nicely in front and then count to two or three before putting him to heel so that you don't inadvertently condition him going to heel as part of the recall; alternatively put yourself to the heel position and praise him.

You can also use the whistle as part of this routine bringing him directly to heel but please establish "come" first as you're going to be relying on that when you formalise your retrieve. Once you do start to use the whistle then pop it in your mouth as you're walking away from your puppy otherwise he may start pre-empting you as you raise your whistle knowing what's coming next.

As part of your formal recall training, ensure that one in three involves you walking back to your puppy's side as you would for the sit-stay so that your puppy doesn't start to pre-empt your training and think that every time you leave him you're going to recall him... hence the reason for establishing a good stay command prior to introducing sit-wait-recall.

At this stage in your puppy's education all recall training is being done in the house or in the back garden; now is not the time to let your puppy off lead outdoors.

Meeting strangers

I can't say enough times that your puppy is your puppy and you decide who he says hello to and who he doesn't, whether that's a human or an animal. Please don't feel obliged to let all and sundry stroke, pet and generally ruin your pup.

Dogs

When you see a dog when you're out and about keep walking. Your puppy may show interest, which is natural; tell him he's a good boy and keep walking and encourage him to do the same.

When he can happily walk past a dog on the field or in the street then it's up to you when you decide he can have a sniff but up until then I wouldn't encourage it. The majority of the gundog breeds are very sociable by nature and need very little excuse to 'party' so they need to learn self control and good manners first.

People

Most people love puppies and really do go over the top when interacting with them causing no end of training and behaviour issues for the owner.

'Way back when' it was considered rude to stroke a dog without first asking permission from the owner; now it seems to be rude for the owner to say that they don't want strangers to stroke their dogs or puppies... ridiculous really when you think about it.

You are going to have to let your puppy say hello to people as part of his education and integration into our society, however, that doesn't mean all and sundry and doesn't mean on his terms. Make a point of not letting him say hello to everyone you pass, say a cheery hello as you walk past and say something like "in training" so you don't feel as if you're being rude, if that works for you.

Every third or fourth person that you meet that shows interest in your puppy ask if they would like to stroke him, or if someone is well mannered enough to ask, then say yes on the condition that they help you train him which means sitting for attention and sitting the whole time the person is stroking him... oh and please don't get the stranger to give your puppy food, please – you'll end up with a dog that once is let off lead, is mobbing every stranger thinking they've got a sweetie for him – it is one of the hardest habits to break so please don't encourage it now.

If you see joggers or cyclists on your travels, and I really hope that you do, take a step to the side and put your puppy in a 'sit'. Keep him sitting as the joggers or cyclists approach and go past... and really go past, not just level with your puppy.

Puppies are predators and even at this young age the instinct to chase and kill is very much there. He won't be that interested in something running or moving fast towards him, although he may be a bit wary 'is that danger heading towards me? Am I prey?' is probably how he would feel, however, when that animal has passed, and bear in mind that we are animals too, then the predator instinct comes to the fore and the chase instinct kicks in... dogs are only ever interested in 'the chase' once something has gone past them and is moving in a direction away from them.

Do everyone a favour, including your puppy, and teach a solid sit-stay around moving objects and animals.

The cone

This is an exercise that is taught in many disciplines but not gundog training, however, I think it should be and I teach it as a precursor to stopping on the whistle.

Get yourself a light cone like they use at football training or similar; a plant pot can work just as well. You can start this once you have taught a solid sit and then increase the complexity over the next couple of weeks.

Let your puppy see you put a treat underneath the cone and tell him to sit; as soon as he does lift the cone up and let him have the treat. Do this many times until your puppy sits automatically. Then hold you puppy with one hand and a foot or so away set up the cone; release your puppy, point to the cone and say "away" as you do so... he'll go straight to the cone and sit.

Once you have trained your puppy to stay, pop him in a sit-stay, walk a couple of paces and put a treat under the cone; return to your puppy, point to the cone and say "away" then follow your puppy to the cone so that you can lift it off for him to get the treat but only when he's sitting.

Keep practicing this, building up the distance that you can put the cone out for your puppy; you can even have someone help you so that you can stay beside your puppy and keep hold of him, just have your helper stay a foot or so away from the cone and once your puppy is sitting by the cone, you can ask your helper to lift the cone off so puppy can get his reward. This is the perfect time to whistle recall him to heel and give him a jackpot, thereby training two really good exercises at the same time.

Pop a treat under the cone while gently keeping your puppy back

Point to the cone with an "away" and release your puppy

When your puppy is sitting by the cone, lift it up and let him have his reward

Whistle sit

By the time you get to the three months mark, if not before, your puppy should be sitting on command every time first time; if he is it's time to introduce the whistle sit.

Every time you tell your puppy to sit follow it up with a single pip on the whistle combined with your sit hand signal (similar to that used by a policeman to stop traffic). It won't take very long for your puppy to put the two together; give him a couple of weeks of whistle conditioning and you'll be able to make him sit just by giving a 'pip' and a hand signal.

Keep training using the word as well though as I can guarantee there'll be lots of times you want your puppy to sit when you don't have your whistle on.

This also applies when you're walking your puppy on lead and you tell him to sit.

At Home

Just as it is, or certainly used to be, with children, good manners really do start at home. If you can instil these while your dog is still a puppy then you can bypass so many training issues and challenges; for example the need to use a long line when training a recall or having your dog ignore you when out and about in favour of going and saying hello to other dogs or people.

By training and moulding your puppy now your puppy will not learn how not to behave and although he may test a boundary or two when he enters adolescence and adulthood, he'll be unlikely to push very hard.

There is one more exercise that I train around the home that will make life easier for you, as a puppy and dog owner. Then it's about slowly stretching your puppy's education by adding duration and distraction to what you've taught him already.

Not you!

This is a great little command to teach your puppy; I use it with mine to teach them not to follow me upstairs or into rooms that they're not allowed in. Later on, when you need to get your dog used to being tied up, and it's something that I recommend you do at some point in the not too distant future, you can just say "not you" as you leave them and it will help them relax.

'Not you' means just that... I don't want you to come with me but you don't have to hold your position as you would with a stay – you're free to move around providing you don't follow me. As humans we like to say something to our puppy as we leave the room (remembering that in the early days that we would only leave puppy in the room if there was another person there to look after him otherwise we would put him in his crate) so 'not you' would fit the bill perfectly.

So, as you go to walk out of the room, say "not you", put your hand in front of your puppy's face so that you're blocking him from moving forward and then move off without him; in time you can just use the hand down towards his face to indicate he's not coming out of the room with you or just drop the communication entirely.

It's much easier to train the 'not you' exercise when you move between rooms with different floor surfaces, for example lino to carpet or at a narrow space; doorways and arches work great.

Go to walk into a room with your puppy loosely beside you and as you cross the threshold reach down with your open hand in front of your puppy's face, say "not you" and push towards your puppy; if he continues walking, gently push his face backwards, say "not you!" and keep walking, go a stride or two and then go back to your puppy, praise him and forget all about going into the room without him, instead head back the way you came.

Build it up so that you can go into the other room, have a walk around and come back out without your puppy following you.

Gently put your hand on your puppy's face and say "not you!"
Keep walking without your puppy and as he pauses, return and tell him what a good boy he is.

Build up to putting a few strides between you and your puppy...

The dreaded dishwasher

So many of my puppy clients have problems with their puppy trying to climb into the dishwasher, hopefully you won't have a problem with this but, if you do have a puppy that simply cannot resist the lure of the smells coming from your dirty dishwasher then this is what you do.

Have a full glass of water sitting on the bench directly above the dishwasher. Leave the door down when you have dirty dishes in there, staying over by the bench as you do. Watch your puppy from the corner of your eyes and when he comes over to the door upend the glass of water into the door; do it silently, do it fast with a wrist flicking action as if you're pouring it down the sink and then put the glass back on the bench.

What we're aiming to happen is that the water hits the open door fast, bounces off the door and splashes your puppy; he won't be expecting it and will jump back... because you're silent and have ignored the proceedings, it will be between the dishwasher and your puppy. If you do this whenever your puppy goes near the dishwasher (set it up a couple of times throughout the day) then the consequence for trying to lick the dirty plates is an unpleasantly wet one.

Just one bit of sandwich... please!

Nope! Absolutely not, no way, no how!

Eating something in front of your puppy will not cause your puppy to become greedy, neither by the way is it cruel or unfair; regardless of how he's looking at you.

The only thing that will make your puppy greedy or hassle you for the food that you're eating is to succumb to the puppy dog eyes and give him a piece; do yourself, your family and any future person that eats around your puppy a huge favour and don't feed your puppy from your plate.

Sorry were you talking to me?

A mistake that a lot of us make a lot of the time, and I do have to plead guilty to doing this at times, is indulging in a constant stream of words to our dogs; things like "oh I think I'll make a cup of tea now" or "is that the time" or "it's getting dark already" or ... well you get the idea.

Then, when our dog looks at us expectantly we think that he understands what we're saying and before we know it we have a severe case of verbal diarrhoea whenever we're around him and, 'because he understands us so well' and because we, as humans, want everything to fit in 'our world', we anthropomorphise him at every turn.

I know you might be thinking "why not?" why's it such a bad thing to chat away to your puppy, that you wanted a dog for companionship and someone to talk to... especially when he looks at you so intelligently, doesn't answer back, responds accordingly and is always there for physical contact... oh and he understands every word.

Well, by constantly talking to our puppy we're teaching him that our voice has no meaning and that he can 'zone out' to it and, if we include his name as well, we're teaching him to ignore that too.

Have you ever lived with someone who walks around talking to themselves, or perhaps you're the one that does it. After asking them to repeat themselves only to be told "oh I was just thinking out loud" you learn pretty quickly to switch off to their ramblings and their voice just becomes background noise.

Welcome to the world of the dog.

If you want to have a conversation with your puppy, or a verbal monologue as he can't answer back, then call him over and then go for it and stroke away to your heart's content as, as far as your puppy is concerned, he's getting masses of praise for coming when you called him and you'll both feel really good.

If he's already beside you then pop him into a sit and then go for it, then he's getting praised for sitting.

Remember your puppy really doesn't understand words, only repetition and association: basic conditioning, nothing more and nothing less. If you use the same words over and over again your puppy will put them together with what comes next; a bit like training the 'sit', your puppy will learn to associate the word with an action however, he doesn't, and never will, understand 'sit' to mean the whole range of 'sitting' past, present and future, in the way that we do.

Let me give you an example... somewhere down the line I started to say "right then" before I got up and did something; "right then, shall I feed you?" "right then, let's go for a walk" "right then, cup of tea" it now evokes a response in my dogs that is instant – they can be sound asleep on their beds but when I say "right then" even quietly, I get the same effect as a sergeant major shouting "on your feet soldiers", the dogs are up and ready to move, even while they have blurry eyes and sleep lines.

Basic conditioning.

It doesn't matter what words you use either, your puppy really couldn't care less. Providing you're consistent you'll be able to condition him to a verbal command so take time now to write down a list of commands that you want your puppy to be conditioned to and stick them to the front of your fridge or kitchen cupboard.

As a bit of fun I train my dogs to get up and walk out of the room whenever someone says "ungawa"; no doubt if you're of my generation you've just got a visual image of Johnny Weissmuller standing in a clearing wearing a loincloth and turning the lions away with a grunted "ungawa". With conditioning any word really will do; it's being consistent that counts.

And remember you don't need words to have a conversation with your dog. Dogs are masters at reading body language and facial expressions; they have to be, they simply haven't got the brain power or the right equipment in their throats for verbal speech.

Human beings have two areas in their brains that allow verbal speech. Broca's area which is associated with the production of language, the spoken word and Wernicke's area which is associated with the processing of the words that we hear. Both areas are named after the scientists that discovered these functional areas of the left hemisphere. Without getting overly technical, these two areas are connected by a large bundle of nerve fibres resulting in the human production and understanding of speech; if any of these areas are damaged then the spoken word is affected, that's presuming of course that the larynx or voice box is working effectively.

Now, because we stand upright rather than on all fours, there is a 90 degree bend in the windpipe, the pharynx; the dog's windpipe has only a slight bend to it. It is this almost right angle bend in the throat that allows the voice box to be lengthened thereby making different pitches of sounds. We also have a rounder, larger tongue than a dog, whose is reasonably short and flat making it impossible to curve around into the necessary position for those complex vowel sounds.

Stanley Coren describes it beautifully in his book How to Speak Dog as "This is much like what happens with a toy balloon. If you blow it up and release the pressure on the opening, the air rushes out silently. Slightly stretching the rubber at the opening to make a narrow slit causes the outward rushing to make sounds, which will vary in pitch as you vary the tension."

It is believed, although not proven, that the transformation of the brain and larynx were by-products or side effects if you like, of humans standing upright thereby separating us once again from the rest of the animal kingdom.

Bringing out the best in your gundog puppy: 10-16 weeks

So far we've been concentrating on puppies in general rather than specifically the gundog puppy... this section is about starting off your puppy gundog regardless of what group he belongs in, so whether you have a Spinone, a Springer or a Labrador we're going to nurture the need to pick something up and bring it back.

Toys & balls

I tend not to start a puppy with balls, preferring little floppy toys like the baby 'farting pheasant', as it's affectionately called, and other small, soft squidgies; the puppy wubba kong is particularly good as it is firm in the middle and has a tail to make it easier to play with and both you and your puppy can hold it at the same time, thereby encouraging your puppy to hold things in his mouth until you ask him to give it to you.

Tennis balls I feel are a little bit too big and tough to start off with and the same goes for gundog dummies; once a puppy is keen on retrieving then I include the pencil puppy dummy and add that to my retrieving toys, however, I never leave the dummy in the toy box as I want, even at this very young age, to differentiate between playtime and work.

I can remember doing a demonstration a few years ago where I took a dog from the crowd and demonstrated how to teach loose lead walking, recall and an introduction to the retrieve. The little dog was a star doing everything I expected right up until the retrieve. I sent him out for the dummy that the owner gave me, he went out like a rocket, picked up the dummy and then lay down and started chewing on it like a bone. "Is this normal?" I asked his owner or words to that effect... "Oh yes, he does it all the time, his favourite game is to chew the end off and pick it up and shake all the sand out".

I did not say and will not write what I thought, but needless to say it was not complimentary: dummies are for working, toys are for playing.

Playing fetch

When you first bring your puppy home, or in the couple of weeks just after, the best way to train your puppy to retrieve is by playing fetch.

I tend to do this in the kitchen, or if you have a massive kitchen then in the area where the kitchen units are or in the hall, that way there's nothing for your puppy to run under and if he wants to keep playing the best way is to come back to you. If your kitchen floor is very slippery then you may want to pull a rug in for your retrieving time so that your puppy isn't slipping around; the last thing you want is to put your puppy off playing as he feels unsteady on his feet or hurt him by him skidding onto his side or twanging any of the puppy-loose ligaments.

Stroke and praise your puppy for coming back

... the toy really isn't important – at the minute that is!

If he doesn't want to give up the toy revert to your 'leave it' command

Sit on the floor with your back against the cupboards having first picked up any toys and closed the crate door if that's in the same room. Have your puppy with you, either by your side or preferably sitting between your legs (as that's where he'll want to return to) and wiggle the toy around to get his interest; toss it out in front of you, no more than two or three feet (hence using the word toss rather than throw) and say "go get it" as your puppy bounds after it.

Encourage your puppy back to you and give him lots of praise and loads of strokes, totally ignoring what he has in his mouth. At this point I'd be saying "is that for me", "bring it here", "what a good boy you are"...

Gently take the toy off your puppy saying "give" or "dead" or whatever word you're going to use to mean hand over what's in your mouth... if he snatches or goes to jump up then 'gasp' and do your 'shocked and surprised' face; when he backs off praise and stroke him and toss the toy again.

Do this two or three times and then give your puppy the toy to play with; if he knows he's going to end up with the toy as part of the game he'll be even more keen to bring it back.

I know I'm using lots of words, and that I advise against it for everything else, however at this 'baby' stage what I'm doing is conditioning 'bring it here' and 'get it' which will quickly turn into 'get on' when we formalise the retrieve.

Why not start with 'get on' is no doubt going through your mind... well, this bundle of fluff is first and foremost a pet. Even in the height of the shooting season I won't go out more than once a week, some weeks possibly twice; that means the rest of the time he's a pet.

I'm a great believer in playing with toys and having fun, it keeps the dog motivated and 'fresh' and if I only ever teach a formal "get on" then I have no way of doing a play 'go get it' kind of retrieve where I want my dog to run around like a loony shaking a toy about.

Playing catch

Once your puppy has developed a bit of co-ordination in relation to toys then playing catch is a fantastic game to play; it teaches steadiness, encourages play with you and is excellent for teaching a nice delivery. As an aside, and so that you appreciate how good this little game is... I teach it to adult dogs as a way of building motivation to please the owner, to introduce steadiness, and for dogs that don't want to either put the retrieve item in the hand or don't want to come back with it.

With your puppy in front of you, hold the toy at nose height (but not too close to them) and say "ready, steady, catch" and as you say 'catch' toss the toy so it does a little arc landing where your puppy's mouth should be... and I say should be as your puppy will probably have danced around and will have moved out the way.

Keep trying until your puppy can catch the toy and as soon as he does go into the "is that for me", "bring it here", "what a good boy you are" routine.

In time, sit your puppy up in front of you and draw out the time before you toss the ball for him, thereby teaching steadiness... so "ready" pause "steady" pause "catch", "yay, what a good boy, bring it here" if he catches it, or "is that for me", "bring it here", "what a good boy you are" if he doesn't.

Playing catch is all about steadiness and delivery

Regardless of how old your dog is, please don't throw the ball high enough to make all four feet come off the ground as you can do so much damage to their backs as they flip around trying to catch it – as a very young puppy the front legs shouldn't be coming off more than an inch or two... unlike young Ziggy, above, who used to try and catch the ball with his paws!

Every retrieve is to the hand

Even at ten weeks old you can teach your puppy to deliver to hand. When playing fetch or catch and your puppy brings you something back, or even when your puppy wanders over to you with a toy in his mouth, praise him for holding the toy and encourage him to 'show off' and 'preen' by stroking him as he circles in front of you... then very gently hold the toy and encourage him to the front of you and take the toy.

Once you have taught your puppy to sit, you can tell him to sit nicely in front of you once you have taken the toy – then either give him back his prize or lure him to your side and toss the toy for him.

I have two unbreakable rules in my house in relation to playing fetch and catch; delivery to hand and then sit. Regardless if it's me or my son's friends that are playing this is how it is... 'give' then 'sit'.

Remember that if your puppy is a little reluctant to give up his toy after you've asked for it, you can always raise your index finger, as you did when you taught 'leave it' and your puppy should hand it straight over!

The puppy retrieve

Once your puppy is happy playing in the kitchen with you and you've taught 'go to heel' then pop your puppy to your heel position prior to playing fetch.

Crouch down or kneel beside your puppy and hook a finger under his collar so that you can restrain him but without putting pressure on his neck; toss the toy and as it lands, or slightly before, remove your finger and say "get on"... you know your puppy is keen to go as you've been playing for the last couple of weeks and your puppy will be familiar with the word "get".

After half a dozen retrieves, not all at once I hasten to add, it's time to introduce the 'wait' command. Set up your puppy as before and this time pop him in a sit by your side.

As you go to throw the toy say "wait" and, after throwing the toy, count to three prior to sending your puppy with an excited "get on".

If he gets up before sending him for the toy (casting him off) then just pop him back into the sit position, say "wait" then send him.

If your puppy gets it wrong it's not the end of the world...

give him a stroke, set him up and send him again...

Stay positive - he will get it right....

At home with the Adolescent: 4-6 months

Congratulations, you no longer have a puppy at home; you have an adolescent.

Adolescence is often referred to as the juvenile period or having a juvenile dog at home and although we tend to link adolescents and teenagers in the same group, they are quite different which is why there is a different section on teenagers.

The easiest way to think of it is by looking at humans as we've all been through it, and then hopefully it will make more sense... adolescence is something that the body, and the mind, go through in relation to hormones as a preparation for the teenage years, a gradual pulling away from parents as friends start having more influence.

The same can be said for your puppy, sorry dog, as he enters his adolescent months; depending on breed he can start behaving as a juvenile a little bit earlier or a little bit later but it's generally thought that anytime between 16 and 18 weeks marks the start of your puppy being a young adolescent; a juvenile; an 'inbetweener'.

Just like with adolescent human friends becoming more important to them, so too will other dogs hold a great interest for your adolescent dog as he'll want to go off and play with them; that doesn't mean you let him, in fact the opposite is very important during these next few months as not only is this known as the play instinct period, when play is high on the agenda, but it's also categorised as the flight instinct period – the time when your dog is most likely to take off. Sorry, I need to repeat that....

This is the time when your dog is most likely to take off...

If you've been following this book, been interesting to your puppy, trained a recall (both the 'come and sit' exercise and the whistle recall) you should progress through the next couple of months relatively unscathed, especially if you've been a good leader within the home too.

If you haven't been, or if you feel that things are unravelling for whatever reason, or if you came to this book late then you may want to get yourself a copy of The Pet Gundog, which kind of runs parallel to this book but presumes no previous training, or very little, in the adult dog and so approaches things slightly differently...

The other major thing that is going to happen in your dog's life during this period is that his adult teeth come through, and I hate to say it but if you think puppy teething was bad then take a deep breath because this is when your dog needs to really work his jaw.

He'll be teething until he's around ten months or so which is when the teeth are set in the jaw and the jaw, and his mouth, start to settle down; until that time please give him access to hard chew toys or antler chews which as you may guess from the name are quite simply antlers (see useful websites). I tend to give them to my dogs after they have eaten as that is the natural time that they'd want to gnaw on something after eating the meat.

Of being consistent, insistent and persistent

As you might guess, this is the time when your young dog is going to test the boundaries; more than he has so far.

You've spent a lot of time training various obedience exercises and starting to mould the dog that you want; don't throw it all away now by thinking 'been there done that, good manners and basic obedience taught.'

This is the time when we're so proud of what we've achieved with our puppy and we are getting told by all and sundry (or at least we should be) on what a good job we've done... and quite rightly so – you've put in the effort, you should be reaping the rewards.

However, you've got a way to go yet... through adolescence and the teenage months before you can breathe normally and start exercising those smug muscles, so no 'resting on your laurels' as they say.

And do you know the easiest way to throw away all that hard work? Yup, you've got it, by not being consistent, insistent and persistent; the three things that if you let slip at home will absolutely wreck your recall.

Just imagine for a minute that you're your dog. You've just been told to go on your bed and as you're almost there you get a whiff of a chew toy; you're fairly close to your bed, in the general proximity of it, so you settle down to eat your toy. Your owner comes into the room a minute or so later, see's that your settled, says "hey good boy" and wanders back out again... you have just learned that a) 'go on your bed' means go to the 'bed area' and b) that you get praised for not doing as you've been told... oh and c) that your owner doesn't mean what he says. Repeat this scenario often enough and you'll get...

Peep-peep peep-peep. You've heard the whistle and you're heading back to your owner, hang on a second, where did that smell come from, best investigate as, to be fair, you've started to do as you're told and that's what you get praised for at home.

Without over humanising the whole thing and giving your dog a higher intelligence that he doesn't possess, this is what happens when you're not consistent, insistent and persistent. If instead your owner had followed you into the room as they told you to go to your bed they could have insisted that you got there and settled down; if they'd been inclined, as I would, they would have given you the chew toy to amuse yourself... but the main thing is that as a dog, you would know that you needed to go on your bed.

So...

Be consistent with your commands. Changing them around can cause confusion and if your young dog is confused it's because you're not being clear and if you're not being clear how can your dog follow you? Most dogs will put their heads down and sniff, urinate or freeze if they don't know what to do – they're not being disobedient, well they are, but only because you're not being clear in your leadership position.

Be insistent with your commands. If you've asked your dog to do something then make sure that he does it. That doesn't mean getting all growly or aggressive – if you've told him to go on his bed and he doesn't, then lead him by the collar and put him on there; then ask yourself if you've trained the exercise properly, if you need to do a bit more training, or even go back a step or two in your training. Never give a command that you cannot insist is carried out.

Be persistent with your commands. Yes I know, you told him to sit stay, he got up, you put him back and he's got up again... put him back again; never give up, to do so will only make your dog persist in doing his own thing.

Remember this is a predator that you're dealing with and they have the hunter's mentality of never giving up; if they gave up hunting because they didn't catch anything they would die...

This is why these three things are critical in training a dog; if he thinks he's going to get away with something he will try to; if he thinks you're going to give up (and he will be able to smell and see by your body language that you are) then he won't... heed the phrase 'the tenacious terrier'.

Taking it further...

You've taught your young dog so many things already; at that young age he really was a little sponge, not only able to take it all on board but wanting to – that thirst for learning will never be repeated. Although you'll still be able to motivate your dog into wanting to learn something new, that 'need to learn' will start diminishing as your dog goes through more important phases of cutting the apron strings, and if he was still in the wild (and the instinct is still there), of leaving his pack and setting up a new one.

Just because we taught the basics doesn't mean they can't be extended or improved upon; in fact the only thing that will really stop you taking it further with your dog will be time or imagination... to help you with both all the training in the 4-6 months sections can be done in the house or the garden and can be done for five minutes at time, as well as some detailed exercises to follow.

Each exercise is designed to improve and extend what you have already taught but the key is to get the foundations absolutely solid before moving on; there's no point in doing your stay training with distraction if your dog cannot sit still for 10 seconds, so common sense must reign and only add in an exercise when your dog is ready to progress.

Walking on a loose lead

Hopefully by the time you get to four months old you've got the loose lead walking cracked; if you haven't or if you find that all of sudden your dog is trying to get ahead of you, then here's a routine for teaching the adult dog how to walk nicely... if you don't need to use it then please don't – this is here as a 'just in case'.

If your dog starts to move ahead, step back giving the lead a quick double flick/a couple of fast gentle tugs, at the same time as turning 180° away from your dog to walk back the way you came giving your dog no choice other than to come with you... only when your dog is walking nicely do you talk to him.

To go back the way you came you can either repeat the exercise if your dog's ahead of you, or left turn and left turn again, walking across the front of your dog (rather than around him) which will encourage your dog behind the leg.

If you do the left, left turn please make sure your legs are straight and you're taking little strides – so you're almost shuffling towards your dog, that way you'll be barging him out of the way rather than kneeing him or knocking him off balance (which we don't want). You're looking to do what another dog would which is barge him out of the way, also, because you're walking across the path of your dog, you're communicating that you're important enough to do so.

Repeat the above step as many times as it takes to get your dog walking with you on a loose lead - the first time may take a little while. Don't continue with your walk until your dog is walking nicely... remember it's the behaviour that brings the reward and in this case going for a nice walk with you is the reward.

Always, always, always return to a loose lead. After every correction bring your dog back to a loose lead.

Before we go any further however, you need to be conversant with what I regard as a flick (or a gentle tug if that's easier to get your head around). Think about flicking water off a paintbrush after you've cleaned it; it's a fast downward flick, the emphasis being on fast rather than hard... that's the flick you use as a consequence for your dog. By being fast rather than hard or pulling, you're mentally pulling your dog up short; you're not trying to hurt your dog or be mean to your dog, just pull him up short so that he knows in no uncertain terms that he has just received a consequence.

Walking off lead

At some point in the next couple of months you're going to want to be able to walk your young dog off-lead and to heel without him taking off. It's a lot easier than it seems, the key funnily enough, is teaching your dog to always walk on a loose lead. If your dog is used to being by your leg without any pressure on his neck, he won't notice the difference when the lead is dropped.

This is the time when you find out if you've been consistent with your young dog walking to heel and if you've been engaging in your training.

The first thing is to find a secure place where you want to train off-lead walking and I would suggest, as with everything, your back garden or driveway, if you have one, is the best place to start, however, if you haven't found a secure 'away from home' place to walk your dog now is the time to find one as, as well as teaching off lead walking over the next couple of months, you'll also be wanting to introduce playtime away from home.

Make sure that your lead is in the hand closest to your dog and when he's pootling along nicely to heel, very quietly drop the lead and let your dog drag it behind him, talk to him as you go – you want his attention on you and not on some bunnies in the hedge.

After a couple of paces do a little left turn, tell him to sit and pick up your lead as you bend down to praise him and heel him away.

Build up to doing more paces before doing your left turn and then build up the number of paces between your left turn and your sit.

You can do the same to the right, remembering to lower yourself slightly to encourage your youngster around the turn with you, once you've straightened up then get your dog to sit and, as with the left turn, pick up the lead as you bend over to praise him.

If your dog gets a little bit too far ahead you can stand on the lead as part of your normal stride which will slow him down by one stride length or pick up the lead, do a double flick and change direction; when he's walking nicely again drop the lead and then do your left turn and sit.

In time you should be looking to introduce the about turns while your youngster is dragging the lead, but bear in mind, as with any exercise that you teach, little and often will get the best results so try to do this three or four times on your walk.

STAY!

We're doing stay again? But we've already taught this...

Yes, we've taught the basic 'stay there until I return' with you leaving your dog either by going out to the side or out to the front; the foundation of all stay training, but now we're going to extend it and make it more challenging.

Take it slowly and take it steady and don't put any pressure on your young dog; this is training to take you from four months to six months – you have plenty of time.

Remember at the beginning of each exercise give a clear stay command and hand signal, at the end of each exercise count initially to three building up to ten, before you release your dog; you can release him by giving him a stroke, a treat, having a play or heeling him off the mark and then making a fuss.

There and back again

Is, as you may have guessed, walking away and leaving your dog, getting to a set point in your mind (could be 5 paces or 50), doing an about turn and returning to your dog's side.

One of the problems that I encountered when I trained Bart (Ziggy's uncle) was creeping or standing up and readjusting himself and then sitting back down before I turned around and looked at him... not the biggest problem in the world, however I was doing obedience trials and competitions at the time and he would lose all his marks.

The way that I got round it was by using a little handbag mirror; you can use this or any little mirror you can slip in your pocket. As you walk away from your dog use it as you would a car mirror to see over your shoulder and check what your dog is doing; the second he moves go back to him and put him on the spot you left him on.

He'll soon realise that he can't get away with anything, even a little bum shuffle, and will stop doing it – remember he's an animal and all animals, regardless of species, will only continue a behaviour if it benefits them.

Rather than using a mirror you can set your dog up so he's facing a glass door and you can see his reflection as you leave him – training in the garden facing French windows works a treat.

Halfs and quarters

Walk away from your dog in a straight line, turn left after 5-10 paces and start walking a circle with your dog at the centre; as you get parallel, after a quarter circle, to your dog return to your dogs side. Repeat to the right. Build up to walking half a circle before returning to your dog. This little exercise will get your dog used to you moving around during the stay and returning on a different path.

You can also hold onto your lanyard if you've trained your dog really good focus using that method, as it will keep his eyes on you rather than looking around for other interesting things.

The circle

Start as if you're going to do a quarter or a half circle but instead continue all the way around stopping when you get in front of your dog again.

This is to teach your dog confidence when you go out of sight. You need to decide if it's acceptable that, when you're out of sight your dog gets up and turns around to see you rather than just looking over his shoulder.

If it's acceptable fine, if not you need to gently escort your dog so he's facing the original direction and repeat the exercise, maybe making your circle smaller and reassuring your dog with an extra 'stay' command as you move out of his field of vision.

For me, I would always correct as stay means stay, regardless of where I am, also, when we get onto the more advanced training (in The Advanced Pet Gundog) you're going to want to be able to put a dummy behind him whilst he's still sitting facing forwards.

Being silly

There can be no greater way of training your dog to be steady in a stay than being silly; apart from that it's really good fun and if you're training with a mate you get to have a laugh at, and with, each other. Only your imagination will hold you back.

Things that I do to train steadiness, with my dogs and with the groups that train with me are... jumping jacks, jogging around the dog, touching toes, sitting on the ground and clapping my hands and knees; in groups you can be a lot more inventive and we jog between and in front of the dogs, do a bit of highland jigging, playing pat-a-cake with each other and stand around gossiping and laughing.

The feint

When you return to your dog don't stop beside him, instead repeat the stay command as you get level and walk straight past him stopping about 5 paces behind. Return to your dog's side, or not it's really up to you, you can go stand in front of him again and repeat the exercise without releasing him in between. This will teach your dog to wait to be released rather than presuming he's going to be able to get up when you return to him.

You could also combine your stay training and your off lead heelwork by leaving your youngster's lead on as part of the stay, and as you walk back to his side from behind him, quietly praise him, pat your left leg and calmly say heel and encourage him off the mark; go a couple of paces, turn, sit and praise.

Stretching the stay

Both the distance and the duration. Walk away for five or so paces and turn to face your dog. If your dog can happily do a thirty second sit stay then after twenty seconds repeat the stay command and take two steps back. After ten seconds repeat the stay command and take two steps back. After another ten seconds repeat the stay command and take two steps back. After another ten seconds repeat the stay command and move forwards towards your dog to the original starting stay position, after another ten seconds return to your dog; this means your dog will, in total, have done a one minute sit stay.

This will very quickly not only increase the time and duration of your stays but will also help your dog to focus on you and not let his mind wander as he'll never quite know what you're going to do next.

You can do it in increments of five seconds, twenty second or five paces it really is about evaluating what your dog is comfortable with at this moment in time and slightly stretching it.

If your dog does get up then you know you've done too much too soon; set your dog up and do a 'baby' stay so that your dog gets to end the session with praise.

Recall to heel... on the move

You trained your puppy to come to the heel position when you blew your recall whistle; you also trained your puppy to walk to heel. Now you're going to train your young dog to combine the two... come to heel on the whistle whilst you're on the move; cool, huh?

With your dog on a lead, and it needs to be a fairly long lead, 6ft minimum; leave your dog in a sit-wait and walk to the end of the lead. As you reach the end of the lead peep your whistle recall and give a little flick/gentle tug with your lead at the same time; keep walking, pat your left leg and say "heel". That reads as if it takes an awful lot of co-ordination, it doesn't really, just practice.

Do this little exercise on your walks as much as you can to teach your dog not only where the heel position is, but that it doesn't matter what you're doing, the heel position is always the same; by your left leg (unless of course you walk your dog on the right).

Try to alternate this exercise between whistle recalling him to heel and returning to where he's sitting, praising him and heeling him off, otherwise he'll think that every time you leave him you're going to whistle him to heel.

Once you're both comfortable with this little exercise, drop the lead when you leave him in a sit-wait and walk a small'ish left hand circle around him, as you pass him whistle recall (or say "heel") and pat your left leg, he should get up and walk to heel with you. If he doesn't, then simply pick up the lead and encourage him to come with you.

Increase the distance between passing your dog on the circle and whistling him in to heel; also increase the distance between him catching you up and walking nicely to heel, and the time before you give him lots of fuss, so that he doesn't explode with excitement once he gets into the heel position.

As well as conditioning your dog to come to heel on the whistle, please take the time to train him to come to heel when you say "heel" that way if you leave home without your whistle you can still call your dog to heel; the training routine is exactly the same just sometimes you're going to use the word 'heel' to get your dog up from the sit-wait and sometimes you're going to use your recall whistle.

Go Play

As yet your dog hasn't had any time off lead or been away from your side away from the home environment; I always recommend that your dog can either do a one minute sit stay in the garden under distraction, or a thirty second sit stay on a walk, is recalling immediately when you train your recalls (both formally and informally) and is well over five months old before you even think of taking off the lead outdoors.

If you've been following this book and resisted letting your youngster off lead then I must congratulate you; it really is the way to go as no dog under around six months old needs off lead time.

If you've given in, for whatever reason; peer pressure, guilt or trying to run a bit of energy off your dog then I understand, but need to go through some questions... did your puppy or youngster return the first time to you every time you asked him to? Did you let him out of sight? Was he running around sniffing and picking up scent trails? Did he play with other dogs? Did he go running up to people to say hello and get a stroke? If you answered yes to all bar the first one then I suggest you skip this bit and go straight to long line training as your dog has found things more interesting than you on your walk and you need to refocus him before he gets any older; if you answered no to all bar the first one, well done... keep reading.

So this is the moment that you've either been really looking forward to or absolutely dreading; I always feel both when the time comes to let my youngster off lead for the first time.

Sit your dog to heel and quietly, and without fuss, take his lead off. Tell him to wait and walk a couple of paces and whistle him to heel; keep walking for a couple of strides and verbally praise him; give him a pat and release him...

My release command is "off you go, go play"; yes a bit long I know but I've always used it. Find something that works for you and be consistent.

To start off with your youngster probably won't leave your side and that's okay. When he gets into the habit of leaving your side let him go about ten paces away and whistle him back, giving him a jackpot for returning quickly to heel. Walk him to heel off lead for a couple of paces and release him again. Next time you call him to you, heel him off lead then tell him to sit and put his lead on; once the lead is on give him a food reward so that the lead going back on is always a yummy thing to happen.

Over the next couple of months build up the time that your dog is having a play but make sure that your walk starts and ends on a loose lead and you have a bit of heelwork, on or off lead, in the middle as well as some play with you either with a toy or doing some retrieving.

Your dog must return immediately 99% of the time, the other 1% being when he's toileting and you didn't realise.

At this important age it's vital that you do not let your dog out of sight for a minute; if you can't see him you have absolutely no idea what he's doing. At that moment in time your dog is in control of the situation which means you're not and if you're not in control there's absolutely no way you can be in a leadership position... and you may well have thrown away all the hard work that you've done since your puppy arrived.

Even as your dog gets older I recommend that he's kept in sight at all times unless he's been sent for an out of sight retrieve, when he's working under your behest rather than his own.

Not only are there unknown dangers when your dog is out of sight, you don't know where he is; he can cover a lot of ground in a very short space of time and do untold damage... raiding pheasant pens, killing rabbits, worrying or even killing sheep, scaring people – the list really does go on... and it's not about damage he can do to others, what about himself? I've known a dog chase a muntjac deer into the forest and come out with her side gaping open, I've known others to be impaled onto snapped branches, tangled up in barbed wire and others be killed by cars.

Please, please, please - keep your dog in sight at all times

Long line training

If for whatever reason you don't feel comfortable taking your youngster's lead off just now, or if you feel he needs a bit of refocusing on his walks then the way forward is to long line him for a little while; it will give him a bit of time to be in his nose and have a play whilst you still have control.

A long line is a longer, thicker, heavy version of the house line that you may have used when your youngster was a puppy. It can be a bought line from a pet shop which generally come in lengths of 10m and 15m, a lunge line that you use with horses or a homemade one of rope and spring clip attached.

I made my first long line from bale twine when I was 13, it must have been at least 300 yards long as it stretched quite easily from one side of the hayfield to the other – I just tied it on to my dog's collar with a well practiced slipknot and removed it when I put her lead back on. Whatever you use just remember not to tie yourself up in it and never let it lie on the ground behind your legs and, if like my first one it's made of thin twine, wear gloves.

Walk on a loose lead to a suitable field or area where you want to give your dog some freedom. Attach the long line (then remove the lead) and walk for about 50 yards or so with your dog by your side on a loose lead. Give your release command and let your dog out up to the length of the long line.

The line must never have tension; as your dog gets towards the end of the long line, give it a quick flick.

You can then say "Dog come" and bring your dog in to sit in front of you, give a stroke and a food reward before putting him to heel and heeling for a few paces before releasing him to play again or to put his lead back on.

Or you can peep your recall whistle and have your dog come to your heel, reward and walk a few paces before releasing him to play again or to put his lead back on.

Or you can say "Dog this way" so that your dog is heading in the same direction as you but at distance; I tend to use this command if the dog is to the side at distance or behind me. Verbally praise at distance and continue walking with a loose line.

Or you can say "Dog too far" if your dog is too far in front of you and then verbally praise as he comes back within a decent range.

Do the above on every walk for 2 weeks. On the 3rd week drop the line and allow your dog to drag it behind him... not only will it slow him down a bit but if he doesn't respond immediately you can stand on the long line for immediate control. If you feel confident with the recall at week 4, then remove the long line.

If you don't feel confident then replace it with the shorter houseline; as your confidence increases you can start shortening the line so that he just has a short lead attached, that way he can feel the touch of the 'line' and still feel attached to you, otherwise continue letting your dog drag the line behind him until you're confident, as regardless of what you believe, you will be right; if you think he'll return (and you've trained him to do so of course) then he will, if you think he won't then he'll pick up on the weak energy and do his own thing.

Never do long line training in the forest or where there are a lot of bushes as it would be really easy for your dog to get caught up and hurt his neck and back.

Don't be shy with your praise - the more exuberant the better. Don't be afraid to use a jackpot (many treats one after the other each accompanied with a "good dog") when training a recall and always use high value treats.

When you give your dog a food reward, give the treat with one hand and stroke him with the other. Remember he's not allowed to go play again without permission.

Stop!
There are many ways to train your young dog to stop on the whistle, however, my favourite way for training my own puppies is through conditioning the cone exercise; it makes it one big game and removes all the stress that can be involved in other ways of training it.

The cone
So far you've taught your youngster to run to the cone and sit and wait for his food treat to be uncovered so that he can eat it. Now you're going to add the whistle...

Once your youngster is happy going some distance to the cone you can start to introduce the sit whistle

Send your dog as usual to the cone by lining him up and saying "away" as you send him. The second he puts his backside on the ground do a single pip on the whistle at the same time as raising your hand straight up into a policeman's 'stop'; make sure that your hand clears your shoulder to make it easier for your dog to see. Walk over to the cone and give him his treat and tell him what a very good boy he is.

Vary the distances that you put the cone and remember that if you have a helper they can lift the cone immediately after you've blown the sit whistle and your dog sits, then you can recall him back to your side.

Once you've conditioned the whistle sit at distance using the cone you can start to use the pip when you're out and about either on a walk or in the garden, just make sure there's absolutely no distractions when you first start and that when your youngster sits you go to him and give him a treat.

S-t-e-a-d-y

Steadiness is so important for so many reasons; you want to be able to take your eyes off your young dog when he's in a stay without worrying about him

getting up and chasing something, or to take off after a rabbit, or a cat, when you're walking him.

If you are going to take him out shooting then it is imperative that he has self control as there will be an awful lot going on around him an awful lot of the time.

When you can leave your dog in a sit-stay and walk a circle around him, both one way and about turning and going back the other then it's time to start putting down distractions; both whilst he's in a sit-stay and when he's walking to heel.

Introducing the clock

It's time, no pun intended, to introduce you to a concept that I use a lot in training and that is the clock. Based on the analogue clock face you set your dog up in the middle where the pointers come out from and you use the various numbers to help you with your training, whether that's steadiness or retrieving exercises, training within the clock is invaluable.

I always enter my imaginary clock, or not so imaginary if you put pegs in the ground, at the 6 o'clock position so that when I stop in the middle I'm facing 12 o'clock; 9 o'clock will be to my left and 3 o'clock to my right. It is up to you how big a clock you work within; in the early days it will be a small, five paces to twelve o'clock clock, when doing more advanced work it could be as many as thirty paces to twelve o'clock.

As part of your steadiness training, leave your dog in the centre of the clock, walk out to 12 o'clock and put down a toy; return to your dog, tell him what a good boy he is and then go and pick up the toy while your dog is still in the stay.

Build up to being able to walk all the way around the clock leaving a toy at the 12, 3, 6 and 9 o'clock positions before returning to praise your dog, leaving him and then walking around the clock again collecting the toys.

When your dog is absolutely steady in the centre of the clock, then you can place the toys down and keep walking round the clock to pick them up prior to returning him.

Yup, you've got it – when you can do the above it's time to make the clock bigger.

Two balls

One of my absolute favourite steadiness exercises to do at home with a puppy and a youngster is playing two balls. Once you've trained your sit-stay have your dog sitting between you and the wall but slightly off to the side, then throw one ball against the wall and catch it whilst keeping your dog in a sit.

When your dog can remain seated then play two balls against the wall. When your dog can remain seated, kneel down so that the balls are passing in front of your dog's face, allow a ball to drop and so on. When I was a kid the game was 'Big Ben'... Big Ben strikes 10, Big Ben strikes 9, Big Ben strikes 8 and so on, for each number you had to do something different with the balls, for example bouncing them off the ground and catching them, throwing them in the air and so on.

Once you've taught your dog how to play catch, then now and again, you can throw a ball towards him (saying "catch" as you do) for him to catch rather than you. This game really keeps the focus as your dog won't know if he's going to be involved and be expected to do something or just sit and watch.

Advancing the Adolescent Gundog: 4-6 months

Now that we have entered adolescence, your young dog is going to be interested in playing and running, generally away from you... this is the perfect time to formalise the retrieve, without your dog realising it, so that walks are not only fun but they're focussed too.

You'll be surprised, pleasantly I hope, by how much you've done so far with your youngster and now how little you have to do to go from puppy retrieve to formal retrieve. Very little will be about your dog as he knows all that is required to retrieve, most of it will be about adding a bit of finesse to the handling and polishing the overall picture.

However please don't formalise the retrieve if you don't feel ready and please feel free to keep your dog on the houseline, or a long line, to do your retrieving... remember the timings aren't set in stone; some time after four months but before six is ideal.

Formalising the retrieve
The retrieve can be broken into the following exercises; casting off; the return; the present/delivery; putting your dog to heel a.k.a. the finish.

Yup, you've trained your puppy all of the exercises; now it's time to make it grown up and link all the elements together.

Casting off
Sending your dog for the retrieve, or 'casting off' as it's called, can make the retrieve simple and set your dog up to succeed every time or it can make it awkward for your dog mentally and physically.

Line your feet up to where you think the dummy, or toy, is going to land. Place the leg that is closest to your dog slightly further back, about half a pace or so. Put your dog into a 'sit/wait' and hold your dog (either by the line or by having a finger under his collar) while you throw the dummy, as it lands say "mark". Give it a second or so and send your dog saying "get on" with an outstretched arm... remember to stay as upright as possible and keep your arm out until your dog's run well past it - keep your weight over your front leg which will encourage your dog forward.

As the dummy hits the ground, the noise it makes will grab your dog's attention and he will look towards the sound and hopefully see the dummy. By saying "mark" as the dummy, or toy, lands you're conditioning the action (of focusing on the landing) to a word (mark) that you can use later as a command.

Now you've got the technique, let's look at the mechanics and the psychology of casting off.

Think of your dog, like any other four legged animal, as having the engine in the back. All propulsion comes from the hind legs, whether that's launching itself over a jump or walking sedately to the fire; all movement for the dog starts in the back end.

As you 'sit' your dog think about where you're planning on throwing your dummy, ideally you're looking to have the retrieve item lined up with your dog's pelvis so that when your dog launches himself forwards he's travelling in a straight line rather than having to twist once he gets moving. It's much easier to line your dog up nicely for a memory/dropped retrieve rather than a thrown one but it's still worth doing to save your dog any pulled muscles.

The reason for lining your feet up with the dummy or 'pointing' at the dummy with your feet if you like, is to emphasise where you want your dog to go. In time if you want to do more serious training with your dog starting this now will be a godsend, if you don't want to do anything more serious than retrieve on walks and have fun this will still make it easier for your dog to understand what it is you want him to do.

Dogs are the only animal on the planet, other than humans, that can follow the point. Even our closest relative the ape cannot. It is believed that the dogs have taught themselves, after being around humans in such a close setting, that following the point is a good thing. Their cousin the wolf doesn't follow the point, although when hunting in a pack, the pack leader will communicate his intention through his gaze. Dogs will also follow the gaze or head movement from a human.

So here we are pointing with our hand and our feet at the object of our desire, our weight is over our front leg indicating forward movement and we've lined our dog's pelvis up to the dummy so that when he launches himself forward for the retrieve he's travelling in a smooth straight line.

The return
Because of starting your dog retrieving nicely and enthusiastically so young we really shouldn't need to do anything other than watch him pick up the dummy and return, however, if he's a bit distracted then call him back as soon as he's got the dummy in his mouth; you can also say 'hold' when he picks it up so that you're putting a word on that action.

The present
This is where the 'come and sit' exercise that you were teaching at eleven weeks or so really comes into its own.

When your dog's about six foot in front of you say "come" and put your weight over your back leg and invite him in to your space, tuck both of your hands in between your knees, take the dummy and tell him to sit as you straighten up, bringing your back leg in so you're standing close to your dog rather than taking your front leg back and putting some distance between you.

Encourage your dog in by walking backwards and keeping your hands midline

Take the dummy while he's standing or sitting; the choice is yours

Just so that you know the reason for putting your hands, both of your hands, between your knees as your dog brings the dummy back; we've conditioned your puppy to find your hands with toys at home, whether that's been part of playing catch, fetch or just carrying things around... if we have them to either side of us then he's not going to know which hand to put it in, and we'll be teaching him to go to the side rather than the front.

The finish
Pop your dog to heel and when he's sitting nice and straight by your side praise him.

There you go, the formal retrieve. That wasn't too bad was it? In time you'll be looking to stand up straight as your dog comes back with the dummy and you'll also ask him to sit for the delivery prior to taking it from his mouth but there's no rush for either of those.

I still take a standing delivery from my dogs about 50% of the time, however I have a choice and know that I can ask for either as both are trained equally well, so take the time out in the next couple of months to introduce the sitting present.

Having fun and staying safe

Remember that just because you've made the retrieve more formal doesn't mean it has to be without fun; smile at your dog when he's getting it right and frown when he is isn't (although not if he's trying his best, then you take a deep breath and do it again).

Remember that these couple of months in your dog's life are known as the play instinct period and nothing will keep your dog motivated and focused on you more at this time than fun... but remember to keep the discipline and leadership there too.

And try not to overdo the retrieving, not only because you could bore your dog to the whole idea of retrieving, but to protect his joints and ligaments; at six months old he's still very much in his growing phase and all those sharp turns as he picks up the dummy and brings it back can be quite hard on his young body, especially when the ground is hard or very wet.

No more than three retrieving sessions a week which consist of no more than five retrieves in a row... three for me being the optimum; first retrieve is understanding the exercise, with the second retrieve there's a sense of familiarity to the process and the third retrieve is the confidence builder, however make sure you always end on a good retrieve, even if it means making the last one very easy.

The Marked Retrieve

A marked retrieve is, quite simply, a retrieve that your dog has seen thrown and has been given the opportunity to mentally 'mark' where it landed.

You start off by throwing it yourself, having your dog 'mark' it (by saying "mark" as it lands) and then when you're ready sending your dog.

When your dog is confidently and consistently going straight to the dummy it's time to increase the distance that you throw it which you can do one of two ways, by getting someone to help you train (see Upping the Ante) or by walking out.

Put your dog in a sit-stay and walk a couple of paces in front of him; repeat your stay command and pat the dummy to get his attention focussed on what you're doing and throw the dummy as usual. Return to your dog and when you're ready send him for the dummy.

The Memory Retrieve

So far all of the retrieving that we have done with our young dog has been 'marked'. Now it's time to introduce something else.

The memory retrieve is also known as the dropped retrieve and is used, not only to make it more interesting for your dog, but to improve his ability to identify items at distance and, as you increase the complexity of the memory retrieve you further develop his latent learning skills.

Pop your dog to heel and, with your dog, walk out ten or so strides. Pat the dummy and make a brrrruuuppping noise to get your youngsters attention and drop the dummy on the ground. Do an about turn to the left and walk back the way you came.

When you get back to where you started do another left about turn and line your dog's pelvis up with the dummy. When he's straight, pop him in a sit and cast him off for the retrieve as you've taught him.

For this exercise I tend to use a left about turn (left turn, then left turn as described in 'walking on a loose lead') rather than a right about turn. Why?

Well, if you were to do a right about turn as you put the dummy down, as you turn away from the dummy your dog could duck out on the turn and pick the dummy up. This is more likely to happen when doing this exercise on a long line or off lead rather than when training on a regular slip. As always set your dog up to succeed in everything and do a left about turn.

By going back to the same position you're giving your dog a sense of familiarity and, once you've trained this exercise a couple of times your dog will learn to 'put together' the landscape with the dropped dummy so as you turn him prior to sending him he'll pull together the picture he had in his mind as you set off to drop the dummy with the picture of the dummy being dropped. That along with his body being pointed in the right direction will contribute to a focussed, enthusiastic retrieve.

Once you're both comfortable doing this exercise at ten paces increase it to twelve and then fifteen and so on, never increase the distance by more than two to three strides as you're developing a skill and if you increase the distance too much too soon your dog quite simply won't see the dummy and will be reluctant to leave your side or lose confidence on the way and stop. Do this often enough and your dog will lose confidence in your handling ability also.

Just messing about on the river

It's a good idea to introduce your dog to the water sooner rather than later, however, wait until after he's gone through his first fear period which should be over by around 14 weeks; 15 to be on the safe side.

I would also try to avoid introducing water for the first time during his second fear period which is sometime between six and fourteen months, although it does tend to tie in with hormonal surges, so around the time of the first season for girlies and leg cocking for boys.

Try to choose a time when it's not too cold as that may well put your young dog off for life and go for a slow running stream that is shallow and has a good bed; anything that moves beneath your youngsters paws is scary for him so as a first introduction to water avoid anything without a good bed.

Ponds are fine once your dog is a confident swimmer as they tend to drop off from shallow to deep very quickly; bear in mind with ponds that, because they don't flow into something bigger, they do tend to become quite stagnant and can make your dog poorly if he swims in them, either by taking mouthfuls of it while swimming, by giving his coat a lick afterwards or by some 'nasties' being left in his ears.

The sea should be left until your dog is used to water as the smells and sounds can be quite overwhelming... and as for the waves, well the last thing you want is your dog under one of those.

Pick a reasonably warm day when you're not in a hurry and take your young dog down to the local stream. Wear your wellies and when you get there quite simply heel him into the water and stand in the stream doing nothing for a moment or two then get his favourite toy out and have a play while standing in the stream. Take your houseline, or your long line if he's a bit older, to pop on him and while you're standing in the stream throw his toy a couple of paces in front of you for him to retrieve; when he's happy doing this throw his toy from the water's edge and send him in from dry land.

The key is to make it fun, have your young dog deliver the toy to your hand and to keep the play safe; once the confidence levels build then you can start to think about taking it a bit further or a bit deeper.

Training the Teenager: 6 months plus

At some point between now and 14 months your dog is going to go through his second fear impact period. Also known as the fear of new situations period, it doesn't really have a 'set' time frame for arrival... quite simply one day your dog is fine, the next day not so much.

I can clearly remember two of my dogs going through it and although I can't recall situations with the rest I'm sure they must have gone through a milder version.

Angus was around the fourteen month mark when we moved house. We were living in New Zealand at the time and we moved from a rural'ish area to town, or to give a UK equivalent, a large village; it had a busy road not far away, what I would class as a typical UK 'B' road. Many days were spent just hanging around on the corner of our street with Angus while he went through all manner of reactions to traffic... although he'd seen and been walked around traffic it wasn't quite in such volume.

After a few weeks everything was cool for Angus and traffic no longer posed a problem for him. Then one day he almost wrenched my arm out of its socket as he leapt sideways and away from a concrete post; it didn't move, it had always been there but today, for some reason unknown to me, it had become the scariest thing on earth.

Ziggy went through a similar thing when he was around ten months. Always an inquisitive puppy he grew up into a confident and enthusiastic adolescent, always keen for doing something new and even the boring mundane stuff like emptying the washing machine was exciting. That was until one day when I took a shirt out and shook it... all of a sudden it was a monster that was going to eat him – he shot out of the kitchen and stood shaking in the sitting room.

"Here we go again" is what went through my head.

So what did I do? For both dogs it was a case of firstly not making a fuss and secondly desensitising them to the situations. With Angus it was a case of walking ever decreasing circles around the concrete post, a little every day until I was leaning against it; when he relaxed and stopped looking at it out the corner of his eye I gave him a treat, well many treats actually but only when he was relaxed. I also threw treats near the post for Angus to go and get.

With Ziggy it was a case of calling him to me when I was crouched by the washing machine and giving him a treat; taking an item of clothing out of the machine, giving it a wiggle (rather than a shake) and rewarding him for not reacting. I slowly built it up over a couple of weeks so that I could shake out clothes again without him being worried.

It's really important that you don't react to the fear; in the same way you didn't reassure your dog when he was a puppy showing wariness, so too is it equally important now.

Likewise don't force your dog to confront something he's scared about; just be in the moment, be calm, be quiet, don't fuss and get in touch with your 'inner matron'.

The second fear period does tend to tie in with growth spurts and hormonal surges so with dogs watch out for it round about the time that they start to cock their legs to urinate and with bitches around the time of their first season.

Just as this period has no start date, the end date is kind of woolly too so be patient and go with the flow; lead by example and show that there is nothing at all to worry about.

Upping the Ante

I tend not to train the more advanced moves of 'get out' until the dog is seven or eight months old and the 'go back' until the dog is between eight and ten months as, coming from a physical therapies background, I feel that their joints and ligaments simply aren't up to it; rather I spend time really extending the basics in relation to the distance and complexity of the retrieve.

Introducing a thrower

If you have anyone around that is willing to help you train then enlist them as chief dummy thrower.

Have them standing opposite you at a distance (initially only as far as you yourself can throw), have them tap/slap the dummy with their free hand to get the dogs attention and make a brruuuppp bbrrruuuuppp kind of noise and throw the dummy up, underarm. The noise they make prior to throwing it will attract your dog's attention.

This time as the dummy is in the air and the dog is following it with his eyes say "mark". This will improve your dog's timing and marking ability. In your own time, send your dog.

Once your dog is confidently retrieving a dummy from your friend (thrower), have them move further away from you, gradually building up the distance but always bringing it in again after a gap in training. If you increase the distance too quickly your dog will mis-mark it and you'll be setting him up to fail which is the last thing you want. You want your dog to trust your judgement, your training and feel confident and enthusiastic in his retrieves.

Also make sure that sometimes your thrower throws it in different places - to the side of them, in front of or behind them otherwise your dog, the clever wee beastie that he is, will stop marking the dummy fall and instead start hunting around your thrower knowing it's in the general vicinity of them.

When your dog is happy doing one retrieve have your thrower throw one dummy after another; one to each side of them. Send your dog for the second dummy thrown and then after he's retrieved it, take your time to set him up for the first dummy thrown, making sure his pelvis is lined up to the dummy as you place him in a sit.

The reason for retrieving the second dummy first, especially in the early days, is to develop your dog's latent learning skill. The last dummy thrown is the dummy your dog is focussed on and is most likely to get right. It also means he only needs to remember where one dummy is (the first thrown) as he can see, and is focussed on, the second one.

In dogs, humans and every animal in between, latent learning is about learning something and then filing it away for later use. In relation to your gundog it's a quality that is highly valued in working and trials dogs alike and I tend to think of it as your dog taking a Polaroid photo and filing it away for later.

This is another reason why you should try to be precise when setting your dog up to retrieve, it makes it easier for him to find his snapshot of the landscape if he's viewing it from the same position that he took his 'photo' from.

A word of warning when using a thrower to help with your retrieves: don't allow your thrower to whistle to get your dog's attention or shout your dog's name or use words like "here". The first time I asked my husband to be thrower for me I omitted this instruction. My husband whistled then threw the dummy, I cast off my dog and he galloped over to my hubby and did a beautiful present totally ignoring the dummy... hmmmm, let's not do that again!

The clock

Just as you used the clock for your steadiness training, so too are you going to use it for your retrieves.

Heel your dog to the 12 o'clock position and drop a dummy remembering to tell your dog to 'mark' the position; then left about turn and heel to the 6 o'clock position and drop another dummy, again remembering to tell your dog to 'mark' the position; then left about turn and heel back to the centre of the clock face, where you started from.

Pop your dog in a sit beside you (you should be facing 12 o'clock and the first dummy down) and then, when your dog sees the dummy, send your dog.

When your dog has retrieved the first dummy and you've put him nicely to heel, do a left about turn more or less on the spot so you end up facing the 6 o'clock position and pop your dog in a sit. When your dog sees the dummy send him, and while doing so, put the first dummy either under your arm, in your pocket, attaching it to your jeans or drop it quietly behind you.

Initially I would make the clock between 30 to 40 paces across so that when you're in the centre it's about 15 to 20 paces to each dummy. As you increase the complexity of the exercise remember to decrease the distance of the retrieve to ensure your dog keeps a high level of confidence in you and himself.

When you've enjoyed playing with 12's and 6's and feel ready to move on add in 3 o'clock and 9 o'clock. This time walk a large circle with your dog to heel and as you pass the points on the clock face drop a dummy. When all four dummies are down, walk to the centre of the clock and set your dog up to retrieve them in whatever order you choose.

You can also use the clock face to increase your dog's steadiness and rather than walk out to place the dummies down, pop your dog in a sit stay and throw the dummies into position. Return to your dog's side and using the skills you've

learned so far, turn your dog on the spot to line him up to the dummies and retrieve as usual.

Remember to take it slowly and if your dog makes a mistake have a think about whether you've gone too fast for him, in which case go back a step in your training; whether he doesn't understand what's expected of him, in which case go back a step in your training or whether he's dicking about in which case it's back to training the basics of 'come', 'present' and 'finish to heel' and possibly working him on a long line.

The Blind Retrieve

The blind retrieve is, as the name implies, sending your dog to retrieve an item that he hasn't seen being put down. Before you can send your dog to do a blind retrieve he has to trust you that there's something there for him to go find.

Everything that you've learned and taught your young dog has led you to this point; a relationship that's been built on leadership and trust.

Before we go any further with the blind retrieves there's another command you need to train your dog. You'll love this one; it's great fun, although you probably won't love it as much as your dog.

You need to train your dog to use his nose on command. The command or the words that I use are "find it". Other trainers use different words and as always that choice lies with you the trainer, if you want to use another word please do; field trialists tend to use "hi-lost" and the people I regularly shoot with use "where is it" (although it sounds like "weeeeeesit") and others "get it".

Find it!
The easiest way to train your dog to use his nose is to give him something worth using his nose for. For me you can't beat digestive biscuits for this exercise. They smell delicious, they crumble easily and dogs just can't get enough of them, even the fussy eaters.

This exercise is best taught on grass. Armed with a couple of digestives, put your dog in a sit-wait. Walk a couple of paces in front of him, repeat the wait command and crumble a bit of biscuit. Release your dog from the wait and as he comes forward point to the crumbs. As he sniffs the ground say "find it", "good boy find it". Do this a couple of times and then, as he's in his sit-wait, lay out a couple of piles of crumbs a couple of feet apart. Release him from his wait and point to the first lot of crumbs saying "find it" as he's snuffling for them, then, as he finishes, point to the second lot of crumbs encouraging him over and telling him to "find it" again.

Do this little exercise a couple of times a day for a week and at the end of the week you'll have a dog that drops his nose to the ground sniffing when you point down and say "find it". Remember to do it at the end of training or in a different area as your dog will still be able to smell the digestives and may get a bit distracted by them.

Hunting in the home

Take a favourite toy and then put your dog in one room and close the door. If you're at the point where you've trained your dog to sit-stay while you're out of the room do that otherwise leave your dog with a 'not you' and close the door behind you. Go and hide the toy in another room in a very simple place, after first ensuring all the other toys are put away; maybe behind an open door or round the side of the settee... hidden but in view, if you know what I mean.

Return to your dog and let him out of the room pointing to the room you've just hidden their toy in, say "go find it" and walk with them to the room.

Once in the right room, if your dog is looking puzzled say in an excited voice "where's your toy?" he probably won't have a clue what you're saying but will pick up on the energy you put behind it.

Point to where the toy is and say "find it", "find your toy". As soon as your dog finds the toy make a really, really big fuss of him, have him deliver to hand and sit. Then it's back to the room you started in and do the exercise exactly the same, putting the toy in the same position as last time.

This time when you let him out of the room with a "go find it" he'll know where to look, will find the toy immediately and will feel very pleased with himself... you will be following him making sure he goes in the right direction and saying "find it" as he starts to get close to the toy.

It's up to you if you do it again in the same place or set the toy up in a different room. Providing you're consistent in your approach your dog will very, very quickly pick up that when you say "find it" and point, your dog will find something good if he uses his nose in the area that you're pointing towards.

Adding the 'get on'
When your dog understands the 'find it' concept and hunting for a toy it's time to add the formality of 'get on' to the blind retrieve.

Hide the toy as above in its 'usual' spot but have a tiny bit of it poking out from behind the furniture; put another one nearby but totally hidden from view. Heel your dog to a position in the room where he can just make out the first toy, but can't see the other one. Set him up for a retrieve and cast him off, hopefully he'll go straight to the toy and bring it straight back... with a bit of luck he'll have caught a little glimpse of the other toy.

Set him up again and send him in exactly the same way but for the hidden toy, if he doesn't find it straight away play your 'find it!' game so he knows what's expected of him.

In time you can take him out of the room as you set up your toys or dummies and send him for them both as blind retrieves; to start off with though set him up to succeed and only put the toys down in the known hiding places.

Once you feel that you have thoroughly 'upped the ante' and are ready for more, it's time to invest in a copy of The Advanced Pet Gundog and 'go for it'.

Regardless of what you do with your dog, always insist on delivery to hand; standing or sitting, the choice is yours

Out and About

By the time you get to training your teenager you'll have only just started to let him off lead and giving some play time while out walking. It doesn't matter if you wait until your dog is seven or eight months before you embark on this part of his education or even older still. The important thing is that you've trained all the necessary 'bits' to ensure your dog knows what a recall is and that you're confident when you do so.

It is important however, for your dog to have some off lead time to be a dog, get in his nose and have a run. No dog should be kept on lead all of his life; even if he only gets to run on a line, he should experience a sense of doing what dogs do which is run, roll, sniff and be silly... to deny your dog this is, in my eyes, tantamount to cruelty.

Now that doesn't mean it's a free for all as soon as your dog is allowed off lead... nope, it means that even while he is off lead, you are on his mind and you only have to say his name or softly whistle and he's by your side or sitting on the whistle or any of the other things that you ask him to do while he's off lead.

City dogs v country dogs

A friend of mine recently moved to the country from the city and experienced raising his first 'country pup'. Chatting on the phone one day about dogs, as you do, he commented that his youngster wasn't as well behaved or focussed off lead than all his other dogs were; once the lead was off, so too was the dog, in his nose tracing the scent, into the undergrowth – it really was a case of head down and going for it. He came back though, had just as good a recall as his other dogs but just no focus and was very interested in other dogs or people.

And my friend isn't a novice... he's one of the top behaviourists in the country, has a great relationship with his dogs and puts the effort in to training them both as companion dogs and for working trials. It's just that his latest rottie was a country dog as opposed to a city one.

When living in the city, every time he saw another dog he would call his pack over to him and either put them on lead or keep them walking to heel off lead; likewise when there were people around. That doesn't mean to say his dogs weren't allowed to play with other dogs but that he decided when, and, as a first port of call, the dogs came to heel.

This is a great thing to do with your dog as it means his first reaction when he sees a dog or a person is to start heading towards you for leadership and direction as to what to do next.

However, when you live in the country you can go days without seeing a soul on your walks, dogs or otherwise, and then at other times you might see a dog five or ten minutes before you see its owner.

What this means is that you miss out on all the recall training on your walk and of keeping your dog focussed on you as he's regularly being told to do something; sit, come or come to heel.

If you live in the country then you need to make sure that you include the extra training on your walk that you would normally have to deal with if you lived in the city and that means;

> Keeping your dog within about 30 feet of you
> (so that you can react with speed if you need to)
>
> Recalling regularly
>
> Practicing your sit-stays and whistle sits
>
> Taking a toy out with you and practicing your retrieves
>
> And most important of all... do not let your dog out of your sight.

Remember, socialising your dog with another species doesn't mean to take your dog over to say 'hello' as all that will do is ensure that your dog runs over to the horses/ sheep/goats rather than ignoring them.

To castrate or not to castrate... that is the question

It's around now, six months plus, that you'll be receiving no end of useless, uninformed, and out and out bad advice on castrating your dog or spaying your bitch.

You'll hear all sorts of nonsense about doing it now before the hormones kick in, it'll stop him wandering; being aggressive; challenging and all the other rubbish that is associated with entire or intact male dogs.

As for the bitches you'll no doubt be encouraged to spay her before her first season for equally stupid and unfounded reasons.

Your dog's hormones are there for a reason and that is to turn them into adult dogs. Wait until your dog is an adult and have an informed talk with your vet and your breeder and your trainer and then make an educated decision... if you have a vet that is encouraging you to castrate or spay at six months or routinely performs unfounded neutering under a year, all I can say is change vets.

If you've been diligent in your training I cannot imagine that you will encounter any problems with your dog in relation to pushing the leadership boundary and becoming challenging, likewise in relation to good manners and recall; if you do, invest in a copy of The Pet Gundog and work your way through it being absolutely consistent in applying the good manners at home section, then if you're still not happy with your dog get a canine behaviour practitioner out for a consult (see useful contacts), then, and only then, consider neutering for behaviour issues.

As a behaviourist I work with so many dogs that have behaviour problems that have been made worse by spaying and castrating at a young age and could have been resolved by behaviour modification training...

... behaviour modification and a very large dose of common sense that is.

The Shoot and the off-shoots

Some people will go and get their pet gundog puppy knowing exactly what they're going to do with it, others, like myself when I got my first gundog, had never been on a shoot and only got him because I fell in love with his half brother; no doubt if Barney had been a springer or a working cocker then I may well have ended up with one of those rather than my lovely black labrador Bart.

If like me years ago, you've enjoyed gundog training and want to take it further but don't know where to start, I've taken the liberty of copying across the information from The Pet Gundog as it really does cover, at a high level, the things that you can do with your dog when he's older:-

There are loads of things you can do with your trained pet gundog. I can remember when I first got my Labrador feeling totally lost in a sea of jargon... when is a trial not a trial? What's the difference between a scurry and a test? Is there one? What's a rough shoot? The questions were endless... luckily I had a very good mentor and used to bend her ear under the trees waiting for the 'time to work' whistle to go.

As a gundog trainer I regularly get phone calls from people who have got gundogs of 'a certain age', (generally between 6 and 8 months old) saying they want to train their dog to do field trials. They've been to the local game fair and have seen gundogs working in the demonstration ring. "Fantastic" is normally my response, "do you know what a field trial is?"

As we talk it generally transpires that what they mean is they want to train their dogs to retrieve dummies, do scurries and generally have fun with their dog. The information that follows is a brief description of things that you can do with your pet gundog if you feel so inclined.

The Shoot

There are different kinds of shoots and every one of them is run in its own is way. I went on a shoot last season with a couple of the girls who've been training their dogs with me; we were standing out of the way in the picking up line listening to the beaters pushing the birds forward. All three of us had been on different shoots but this was the first time together. One of the girls, who'd only been on one other shoot asked "do the beaters always make that much noise?" "Yes" was one reply, "no" was the other.

I work my dogs at two shoots; one is a formal driven commercial shoot whilst the other is a local reasonably informal driven syndicated shoot (that is a group of people who combine resources to rent the shoot).

Walked up

Many driven shoots have elements of walking-up, especially towards the end of the season when the birds are scarce on the ground. In a walked-up shoot a line of Guns, generally around 100 yards or so apart, will walk along with their gundogs (generally spaniels) flushing birds as they find them. Once a bird is shot, the line is halted while the game is retrieved. At a signal from the gamekeeper the line will proceed and shooting will re-commence.

Sometimes a walked up shoot is also referred to as a rough shoot, however, on a rough shoot the amount of game available is less and sometimes no game is placed down in preparation for the shoot, rather you rely on natural habitat and weather to provide lunch, in whatever form it takes.

Driven

A Driven shoot is the traditional shoot that everyone pictures in their mind when they think of pheasant shooting in Britain, the one that is portrayed on countless paintings. The favourites on a driven shoot are pheasants and partridges, both birds providing their own challenges to the guns. The birds are driven by the beaters and their dogs towards the waiting guns, which are lined up at pegs. It may sound very simple making birds fly up but there is a definite knack to getting the birds in the air at the right time, in the right direction and at the right height for the waiting line of guns.

The shoot is made up of a number of drives, depending on the size of the shoot and can be anywhere between three and eight drives in day.

Beaters, Guns and Pickers-up

As you may have guessed from the above the Beaters are a group of people who flush the game forward for the waiting Guns. On a signal from the gamekeeper, the beaters move forwards with their dogs through woodland or cover flushing or 'putting up' birds in their path. The beaters dog is traditionally the spaniel.

The Gun is the person that shoots the gun rather than the gun itself... complicated but simple! At the beginning of each day, or sometimes each drive, the Guns draw a straw to see which peg, or position in the shooting line, they'll be using. Most Guns tend not to have dogs out with them, concentrating instead on shooting; when they do have a dog with them, the dog will be referred to as a 'peg dog' and is whichever breed the Gun prefers. The Guns do not start shooting until they hear the 'start shooting' marker which is either a whistle or a horn used by the gamekeeper.

The pickers-up and their dogs stand at a distance behind the Guns. When they hear the second whistle they know that the shooting has ended for that drive and they can release the dogs to do their job. The younger or less experienced dogs are generally kept on lead until the second whistle goes, whereas the more experienced and 'steady' dogs are sat off lead by the handler. These are the dogs that are sent for a pricked bird (injured but not killed) before the second 'end of shooting' whistle goes. An inexperienced dog is never sent for a pricked bird as it can frighten the dog and make it apprehensive on game.

The Gamekeeper

Last but definitely not least there is the gamekeeper, who not only organises the rearing of the young birds but deals with the administration involved in the shooting day, from taking the booking to organising beaters and pickers-up and keeping everything running smoothly on the day. It's one of the most stressful jobs I'm aware of as when it goes well no-one comments but when it goes wrong, for whatever reason, the gamekeeper is in the proverbial firing line.

I can remember my first shoot as if it was yesterday. I hadn't really planned on doing anything with my Labrador other than having a really well trained dog. When he was about 5 months old I went on a shoot with his breeder and watched his mum work; that was it I was totally hooked. To see the dogs working in the way that they've been bred to was just awesome. It doesn't matter what discipline I do with my dogs or how much they enjoy it, nothing lights up their eyes in quite the same way as picking up, be that on a shoot or just training with canvas dummies.

Field Trials

Fields trials are serious business and are based on either a walk-up shoot or a driven shoot. They are run by gundog clubs around Britain according to the Kennel Club Field Trial Regulations and are held during the shooting season. Your dog needs to be a pedigree and registered with the Kennel Club.

Nothing is staged and therefore your dog needs to be competent retrieving feather and fur, and, your dog needs to be incredibly steady. Steady enough to walk to heel off lead or sit by your side while guns are going off, dogs are flushing birds, hares are running past and other dogs are retrieving; all without a command being given. Oh, and your dog needs to be silent. Any whining, yipping, yapping or barking and you will be asked to close the gate on your way out.

Field trials can be either one day stakes which normally have between 10 and 16 dogs, or two day stakes which are generally 20 to 24 dog events. All field trials are seriously over-subscribed and so the entrants are decided by a draw.

Apart from the standard of training and dedication involved and the luck being picked in the draw, there's also the travelling around the country to get to the trials as well as the massive expense in doing so. To achieve the heady recognition of owning a Field Trial Champion (FTCh) you need to have won at least three days worth of Open stakes (2 two days stakes, 3 one day stakes or 1 two day stake and 2 one day stakes): no wonder the FTCh on a dogs pedigree is so highly sought after and held in such high regard around the world.

Working Tests

Working tests are fairly serious and are run by gundog clubs around Britain according to the Kennel Club Regulations for Gundog Working Tests (GWTs) and are held throughout the year, although primarily in the summer in preparation for the shooting season. Your dog needs to be a pedigree and registered with the Kennel Club.

Nothing is shot during a working test, although cold game may be used as well as canvas dummies. Mimicking a shoot as closely as possible your dog is expected to retrieve marked and hidden (blind) dummies at distance and over obstacles.

There are four categories of Working Gundog Tests:

Open, which is open to all dogs of a specified breed although preference may be given to dogs which have been placed at a certain level at a Field Trial.

Novice, which is restricted to dogs which haven't gained a place above a certain level in a Gundog Working Test.

Puppy, which is restricted to dogs of a specific breed and less than eighteen months of age.

Unclassified which is open to all breeds but restrictions are determined by the group, club or society that is running the test.

There is a little bit of rivalry between working test handlers and scurry handlers; the working test handlers generally thinking that scurries are for amateurs or that they'll 'break' your dog for bigger and better things.

Scurries

A gundog scurry is a fun event which is open to the general public regardless of breed and ability and can be found at Country fairs up and down the country from local to national throughout the year.

Scurries are a test of speed combined with a retrieve and range from the novice scurry where your dog is timed on picking up two thrown dummies, to the skill stretching pot black where your dog has to retrieve dummies that are coloured like and retrieved in the order of a game of snooker and anything in between.

Although there are generally prizes in the scurries, they really are all about having some fun with your dog. The only pressure when entering a scurry is the pressure you put on yourself.

As you can see, scurries are a lot less formal than the working tests mentioned above, but like most things with your pet gundog, it's your choice in what direction you want to take your dog and what you want to do with him.

About the Author

Lez Graham runs 'Trained for Life' and 'The Pet Gundog' and works full-time as a canine behaviour practitioner and gundog trainer, working with clients on a one to one basis in their homes in and around Wiltshire. Aside from her busy consultancy, she also runs weekly gundog training classes and specialised gundog training days.

Lez has an MA in Professional Practice (Canine Behaviour & Psychology), is a full member of the Canine and Feline Behaviour Association and is a master trainer with the Guild of Dog Trainers.

In 2010 Lez co-founded The Pet and Working Gundog Organisation which was set up to encourage gundog owners of all ilk to spend time training and honing their gundog's abilities, and is an executive and specialist dog handler with the Dog Safety Education Executive (DogSEE) which she co-founded in 2011. Lez is also a tutor on The Cambridge Institute of Dog Behaviour & Training degree programme.

Lez has trained and competed her dogs in obedience in the UK and New Zealand, in Gundog Field Trials in NZ and Gundog Working Tests in the UK; she is an assessor for The Kennel Club Working Gundog Certificate.

Lez lives in Wiltshire with her husband, her son and her two gundogs.

Ziggy at 3 months ...

... at 5 months ...

... and at 7 months.